Endorsements

In Ann Coker's *An Honest Caregiver,* she shares her journey as wife and caregiver to the love of her life, Bill, who ultimately passed away from Alzheimer's disease. It is a story of love, faith, and resilience, capturing moments and memories that both inspire and challenge us to trust God in every season of our lives. Ann's memoir brings to light the everyday struggles and joys of caring for a loved one, sharing her real and raw emotions and frustrations with a touch of humor.

I appreciated Ann's candid retelling of their day-to-day experiences, both good and bad, because it helps us understand the gravity of a caregiver's role and the impact it makes on the lives around them. Although not all caregiving experiences are the same, caregivers will find common threads and glean wisdom from what Ann learned. She shares Bible verses that brought comfort, and how, with the help of the Lord and her family, she found the strength to navigate the unknown road ahead. I highly recommend this book to anyone who is a caregiver or who might find themselves in that role one day. The reader will find encouragement, practical advice, and a friend who wants you to know you are not alone.

—**Doris Swift, host of the** *Fierce Calling* **podcast.**

This memoir is a journal of the experiences of Ann Coker as she was the principal loving caregiver of her husband, Bill, during his years living with Alzheimer's disease. The book is a treasure trove of spiritual examples of how to care physically and biblically for someone gripped in the horrible disease of dementia, and how to victoriously endure mentally, physically, and spiritually the hardship of such care. As I read, sometimes I simply had to stop to digest all the different situations Ann had, especially when she felt she had responded from the flesh rather than the spirit, and how she took her perceived failures to the Lord in prayer for forgiveness and the Scripture for guidance.

At the same time Ann was caregiver for Bill, I was caregiver for my wife who also had Alzheimer's disease. Sonya, was taken to be with Jesus on February 18, 2024, while Bill joined the heavenly congregation on March 7, 2024. Every caregiver will benefit greatly by reading and keeping a copy of this memoir handy for quick reference while traveling the journey with their loved one.

—**Charles Mallory North, Jr.,**
B. Aero. Engr., M.S., M.A. Ph.D.

I have walked the Alzheimer's road with my father, my mother-in-law, and again with my husband. From my experience, stubbornness seems to be a part of the disease progression. Ann's memoir is an honest account of her caregiving experience—right down to mopping the bathroom floor and changing bed sheets in the middle of the night—always giving glory to God for strength, wisdom, and much needed rest. I love this quote: "While facing my fears, my faith stayed grounded in Christ. Nothing could separate me from God's presence—neither my fears for today nor my worries about our tomorrows." I agree with Ann, the only way to face a caregiving challenge is to be grounded in Christ.

—**Elaine Dinnage, mother of three adult children,
Indianapolis, Indiana**

Ann Coker's *An Honest Caregiver* is a book filled with warmth and authenticity. Coker deftly walks a difficult line in this book: she reveals the unique and heart-breaking struggles of caring for a loved one with Alzheimer's without glossing over any details of how it affected her. Yet she maintains an encouraging, hope-filled voice her readers no doubt need. This book wraps caregivers in a hug and says, "You are not alone and it's okay to feel angry and lost." Warmly recommended to anyone who finds themself in the caregiver's role. This book will be a lifeline.

—**A. L. Rogers, writing coach and co-author of**
Rescued for a Reason **and** *Wave by Wave*

Ann Coker beautifully and transparently shares with the world her journey of caring for her husband as he traveled the path of dementia. Having learned of my mother's dementia diagnosis, and although our choice of care for her is much different than Ann's choices, I learned a lot about the process of dementia by reading Ann's book. No one is ever prepared to hear the news that a loved one has dementia. Choosing the type of care to provide for the loved one is an immediate decision that must be made. It is one of the hardest decisions, especially when the best interest of the loved one is the main consideration, but he or she cannot communicate any preferences.

My mother went from diagnosis to hospice care in less than six months. Fortunately, we found an exceptional memory care facility available for her almost immediately, and she is well cared for. My involvement is from 600 miles away, yet I found Ann's book to be most helpful in recognizing the characteristics of the disease and the emotions my siblings and I struggle through. I recommend Ann's book for anyone who is facing a future as a caregiver for someone with dementia, no matter what type of care is chosen for the loved one.

—**Julie McGhghy, author of *Hey Dad, It's Me* and creator of the *Confidence in God with Julie McGhghy* podcast.**

This book will be a great resource for anyone caring for a person with dementia. I have several people in my life who are doing that very challenge effort, and this would help them tremendously. Your questions at the end of each chapter are a good way to connect to the reader. Ann, you revealed how you endured struggles while caring for your husband. But we are confident in God who gives us strength to do the hard things placed before us.

Thank you for giving me the opportunity to read your transcript. I agree with the ending of the book where you talk about how to care for people in this situation. As a quadriplegic, I have several people who care for me, and your list of reminders for caregivers is helpful. These will benefit people who are caregivers.

—**Pastor Jonathan Srock, author, Smithmill, PA**

An Honest Caregiver is the account of Ann Coker, a lady of faith, who openly shared the painful struggles of caring for her husband, Bill, who had changed from the person she knew and loved through the years. Ann's care required determination beyond what seemed possible some days—and some nights! Her commitment is an inspiration, offering hope for success on a difficult journey that taxed her lofty goals.

As I have become the caregiver for my husband in his Alzheimer's battle, I understand what

I could not understand as a child observing my mother's caregiving for my grandma. Now, I acknowledge my need and eagerly seek a mentor's guidance. Ann's book is such a mentor. It has become a steadfast source of encouragement for my tough moments. If you have entered the caregiver role, I urge you to use Ann's story as a help that leads to hope as you face each new day.

—Karen Propst, wife, mother,
and caregiver, Terre Haute, IN

Ann Coker saw her blue skies fade into Alzheimer's grey and hope bounce around like a fishing bobble. Her life wasn't over, for she resolved in her heart and in the sight of God, that this disease would not remove her husband from their home. She would be his caregiver. That's where her book, *An Honest Caregiver*, finds its beginning.

Alzheimer's Disease is but one of the disorders under the umbrella of dementia, and the most common. For anyone who battles thoughts of a loved one having Alzheimer's, or for anyone bobbling on the waters of uncertainty about Alzheimer's, this book is worth the read. For anyone who is or has been a caregiver, I heartily recommend this book by an honest caregiver.

I fall into this third category; I was caregiver for my husband. This book released within me both tears and laughter and yes, precious memories of our final years. Like Ann, although our circumstances were quite different, I refused to allow anyone to take my place. I was the one he needed (even when he didn't know me) and no one loved him as I did.

—**Arlean Selvy, retired publisher/editor,**
Monroe County Beacon, **Woodsfield, Ohio, editor**
of *JBC Bread Basket*, **Powhatan Point, Ohio**

An Honest Caregiver

"You shall do what is right and good in the sight of the Lord, that it may be well with you and that you may go in and possess the good land which the Lord swore to give your fathers."

—Deuteronomy 6:18

An Honest Caregiver
Facing the Reality of My Husband's Dementia

Ann L. Coker

Foreword by Rebecca Coker Gearhart

Publisher
Ann L. Coker

Dedicated to

Rebecca Anne Coker Gearhart, RN
our daughter and joint caregiver
for her dad,
my husband,
William B. Coker, Sr.

Table of Contents

Foreword

My mother phoned, stating she and Dad decided to move to Indianapolis and wanted to purchase a house with my husband, Paul, and me. For two years we had discussed different options, knowing my mom would need help caring for my dad. Suddenly we put preparations in motion, including the sale of both of our houses. The search began and we found a home here that would meet our needs.

No one can fully prepare you for all the nuances of caring for a loved one with dementia or Alzheimer's disease. We read several books to understand the disease process and to know better what to expect. Several well-meaning people told me we would not be able to keep my dad in our home for the entire process. We determined to try to keep Dad at home with us. Everyone's circumstances are different, and this isn't always possible.

Although we experienced difficult times—watching my dad slowly slip away into the recesses of his mind—we could give thanks for much. I am thankful for the home we found that provided a secure place for my dad and where everyone had space of their own. I am thankful my dad remained happy most of the time, and he never became so violent we could not care for him in our home. I am thankful for the support of my husband, and of my brothers who made it a priority to help, including staying at the house when Paul and I traveled. I'm thankful for friends and family who prayed for us, advised us, loved on us, and took this journey alongside us.

Jay Allen wrote the song, *Blank Stares*, about his mother going through early-onset Alzheimer's disease. With his permission, I quote some of the lyrics:

> "It's getting harder and harder to watch
>   you disappear
> Oh if only farther leaving me in tears
> If I could only seal the cracks you're slip-
>   ping through
> Wish I didn't feel so helpless when it
>   comes to helping you
> Hold on
> But I keep holding on
> Every little memory made of you and me
> Every little glimpse of who you used to be
> I know you're still in there

Deep down somewhere I swear I still
  see you
I still see you
Between the blank stares"

Dementia is a long, slow, and difficult process of dying. My dad used to say that growing old is not for sissies. Caring for a loved one with dementia isn't for sissies either. Hold on to Jesus!
—**Rebecca Anne Coker Gearhart, RN**

Introduction

One weekday morning Bill walked into the kitchen wearing only his jockey shorts and undershirt. This surprising scene happened two years after moving to Indianapolis and buying a house together with our daughter and her husband, Becky and Paul Gearhart. Bill held two pairs of socks in his hands and asked which ones he should wear—black or white. My immediate reaction was fearful that our houseguest might find my husband in his underwear. I told Bill it didn't matter; he should decide which socks he wanted. Because he couldn't choose, this didn't solve his dilemma.

I led him back to the bedroom where he again held out the socks. I said, "white," as he entered the walk-in closet where we dress, and he sat on the cedar chest. Unsure where to put the black socks, he handed them to me. To make the routine easier, I laid out a pair of jeans and a jersey shirt for him to wear, while I returned to finish prepping breakfast.

This episode illustrates how Alzheimer's disease affected my husband and how I reacted on the spot. You'll read about our journey and view the stages of dementia caregivers experience. To our family and friends, be warned. You will see Bill as different, radically changed, not how you knew him (or me).

Years ago a dear German friend wrote the following for Bill's birthday:

"Worship the LORD with gladness; come before him with joyful songs' (Psalm 100:2). Dear Bill, how can I read this Word and not think of you? You always have a song of praise and thanksgiving in your heart, which constrains you to serve God with joy and gladness. What a wonderful manifestation of this truth in a person, so that everyone can see. Bill, you are a witness of His love and care for people, and it brings me deep joy and gratitude to know you. May the Lord bless you and keep you! Yours in Christ, Stefanie"

I introduce you to my husband before dementia began to control our lives. Bill grew up in New Orleans, Louisiana, the third of four children by a Mississippi-born hard-working couple holding modest jobs. His father worked in the railroad yard and his mother held a filing job in the basement of Charity Hospital. In spite of the family's meager income, all three sons graduated from college.

Bill stayed home to attend Tulane University, earning a BA degree with a major in philosophy and a minor in English. He graduated in 1957, also the year we got married in Mobile, Alabama, after I graduated from Murphy High School.

Four years prior, Bill, as a senior in high school, distinctly heard God's call to preach. Upon graduation from Tulane, Bill's Uncle Bud, a Methodist pastor, helped him secure an appointment as a supply pastor of a small church in North Biloxi, Mississippi.

Bill later received a BD (bachelor of divinity) and ThM (master of theology) from Asbury Theological Seminary, Wilmore, Kentucky, in 1963 and 1965. Then at Hebrew Union College in Cincinnati, Ohio, he earned a PhD in 1973, with a major in Hebrew Linguistics. During those years, Bill also pastored churches, providing "room and board" for our growing family of three sons and a daughter. For two years Bill taught at Asbury Theological Seminary and then moved to Asbury College (University) as professor of Bible and Greek until 1989 when he accepted a pastorate in Terre Haute, Indiana, at World Gospel Church (WGC).

There was a drastic contrast between Bill as professor and pastor and how later dementia ruled his brain. After 19 years as pastor of WGC, Bill retired in 2008. In July of 2010 he spent 24 days in the hospital with Legionnaire's disease. This time of deprived oxygen may have exacerbated the onset of Bill's dementia. In 2017 we moved to Indianapolis into a home we bought with our daughter and her husband, Becky and Paul. Bill's new neurologist in Indianapolis referred to Bill's dementia as Alzheimer's disease and updated his medications.

While I relate the various stages of dementia Bill traveled through, I also share what I learned about myself. This is my story—how I cared for my husband. If you are now a caregiver for a loved one or soon to see yourself in that role, our journeys may connect. Thus, in the back of this book I've included a list of several insights useful for caregivers. These were a part of my personal journey, so they may vary with other caregivers. Each experience is different.

Early in the process Bill understood he had memory loss, affecting his knowledge of names and events. Gradually losses accumulated, also the ability to care for himself. As his caregiver, my most profound loss became Bill as he used to be; my expectations from him no longer held reality. Other substantial losses I sensed deeply were the loss of our former intimate relationship, my independence and control, along with loss of connections with family and friends. What I hope to convey is how we lived this out in daily interactions.

I chose the cover art of a double-sided tree, because it depicts well what dementia is compared to what life was before dementia. One side is baren and fruitless, while the other side is bright and fully alive. Ambiguous loss is seen in this image: being here but not present.

Every good skit, play, story, or book needs a beginning, middle, and ending. The beginning of our caregiving story started with Bill's Legionnaires' disease in 2010. While writing in my journals about the messy middle of about ten years, I did not know how or when this story would close. The final stage was brief. The end came on the seventh of March 2024 when Bill, after two weeks of in-home hospice care, breathed his last.

A new chapter began with my grief journey.

—Ann L. Coker

PART I

In the Beginning—
Our Lives Changed

"Thing" became the chosen word when specifics escaped Bill. If he couldn't pull up the correct word, he called it a thing, whether an object or an event. He forgot common words and their meanings. While our son John visited us in Terre Haute, Indiana, Bill asked him to take a thing from the kitchen cupboard, meaning a cup for coffee.

Our family recognized the first signs of Bill's dementia after his 24-day stay in the hospital with Legionnaires' disease (July 2010). I acquired a new appreciation for oxygen, as pneumonia depleted needed oxygen from every cell in his body. The hospital's first x-ray showed both lungs as fully white, like a snowstorm. For an extended time, he was given a high dosage of sedative. Although this combination satisfied me as the onset of Bill's dementia, none of the doctors agreed. After several tests, his first neurologist attributed the cause of memory loss to hardening of the arteries. His second neurologist in Indianapolis gave a more specific diagnosis of Alzheimer's disease and explained that the Legionnaire's may have exacerbated the onset of Bill's dementia. The how and why remained a mystery.

During Bill's extended stay in Union Hospital, Terre Haute, Indiana, my time back and forth in the car gave opportunity to thrash through the dilemma. I rehearsed what the doctors said and how Bill slowly responded to treatment. Confident those were not Bill's final days, I read to him from the Bible, mostly Psalms and Proverbs which spoke to his faithful ways, his life of integrity. My sustaining verse through those troubling days became Psalm 34:8. "Taste and see that the Lord is good; blessed is the one who takes refuge in him."

God's presence proved real, especially in anxious moments as I cried out to God, waiting for doctors' visits and connecting with family and friends. Bill was intubated and sedated in his room on the second floor in ICU, yet God's presence resided in that strong tower. I reminded God of Bill's faithfulness, his call in ministry, and his commitment to truth.

Members from our church were also sick and two died during Bill's stay in the hospital. My questions in prayer to God asked why Bill escaped death. The answer connected with God's sovereignty. Bill's recovery happened *not* because *we* prayed, but because of God's unmerited grace. God allowed Bill to live by His mercy, not because we met any requirements. Like children learning to "trust and obey," we experienced God's faithfulness.

Bill returned home and stayed on oxygen for a short period. Even though it was summer, Bill said he was cold and wore a sweatshirt and wool scarf as he sat on the screened-in back porch soaking up the sunshine. Family members visited and we held cautious conversations around the dinner table. Although glad to be home, Bill still exhibited side effects of the pneumonia. Too many uncertainties clouded my thoughts.

The first sign of dementia involved word associations. When he forgot the name of a person, even family members, Bill got creative. Before one visit from our triplet great-grandchildren, he repeatedly asked me their names. Even knowing that repetition is a sign of dementia, I still became irritated. Several times I replied, "Ethan, Naomi, and Levi." Bill devised names of his own: Ike, Mike, and Mustard. When the kids arrived, they liked and chose their names. Of course, Bill didn't recall which name belonged to which kid; he just grouped them. They didn't mind; it was fun.

While preaching for a friend, Bill informed the church attendants about a famous revival of the past. It's known as the "haystack revival." Not able to think of the right words, Bill called it a revival started on "a pile of straw." I cringed inside, assuming his dementia now became public. Our daughter and two of her children attended and heard the sermon, so afterward I pointed out this example of memory loss to our granddaughter. Chrissa replied with compassion, "But Grandpa's vast knowledge of words gave him a good substitute."

To be more attuned to Bill's needs, I resolved to reflect in word and deed the true picture of a biblical wife. This began at home, to please my husband. Instead, after a failure I often berated myself, reflecting poorly on my care. It didn't make sense because after his hospital stay, we were drawn closer and became more consistent with praying together each night.

Stopping to observe my spiritual and mental progress, I was surprised at times to admit how my attitudes changed from courageous and honest to being fearful and irritated. My aim to live in victory moment by moment was too often flawed. Life worth living depends on trust and continuous effort. I needed a quiet confidence. Surrender involved a daily choice to trust God, not being dependent on my own understanding of situations.

Even though Bill had retired from the pastorate, we maintained friendships developed at World Gospel Church (WGC) and Free Life Community Church (FLCC). One evening John and Connie K. treated us to dinner in Terre Haute. While relating Bill's hospital stay, John reached across the table to touch Bill's hand and expressed how he ached when he first got the news. John said, "I've never prayed so much in all my life." I thanked John for that sincere support of Bill and his ministry. Another night we invited friends from WGC for dinner, and their conversations deposited goodness into our memory banks. We also held a dinner party when Stefanie, our German friend, visited. We included Jim and Barbara W., Mallory and Sonya N., and Andy and Mimi M., friends when Stefanie attended Rose Hulman Institute.

During these early months we noticed further indicators of the downward spiral of Bill's memory. Talking with friends, Bill lost track of subject matter. He interrupted with something unrelated and soon repeated it and that embarrassed me. When family members visited, he had little interaction, staying in his study on his computer. Not working on sermons, he simply looked at funny episodes online or played solitaire. I didn't like this and invited him to join us. He still entertained the great-grandkids with his silly facial expressions, teasing the older ones and holding the younger.

Preaching and Serving

Bill continued to accept invitations to preach and serve as clergy on Emmaus Walks. He substituted for pastors on vacation, and sometimes he repeated illustrations. During one message he stumbled over the Bible text, trying to quote it from memory. Immediately I asked the Holy Spirit to bring the verse to his memory. God answered! Yet most messages had few memory blocks.

Bill led a mid-week Bible study at FLCC. When he showed memory gaps, we eventually came up with a substitute. We bought a tape recorder and played sermons from previous years at his former church, WGC. People continued to attend and discussed the topics.

When Bill spoke, we often heard repetitions, forgetting what he'd already included. While preaching, he forgot he'd given a point and repeated it again, out of order. Bill's last sermon was a Good Friday community service held at FLC Church. I asked a friend from WGC if she noticed Bill's repetitions of words and subjects. Yes, but she was not concerned; instead, she appreciated hearing him expound on God's Word.

In September of 2013 Bill had eye surgery at Midwest Eye Institute in Indianapolis to remove floaters from his right eye. After two days in Indianapolis, we returned home, physically and emotionally tired from the procedure. I applied drops to Bill's eyes and he got impatient as we talked about restrictions. The bottom line was fear.

Bill took a while to recognize he wasn't doing well as he worked Emmaus Walks. Such as the time he forgot his place and repeated a section of his talk at a team meeting. He found out later, and did not want to embarrass himself or those in attendance. He made a difficult decision not to accept further invitations to join a clergy team.

Another decision: he canceled his part in two marriage ceremonies planned for April and October of 2015. During a previous wedding he had repeated the bride's vows and didn't want that to happen again, spoiling the ceremony. This we recognized as a new stage in the process of warped memory. He personally faced facts and admitted it would not get better. Agreeing with his choices, I didn't want anyone to be embarrassed, especially Bill. God would see us through this, but we also needed medical advice and counsel.

During an Easter dinner at our daughter's home in Indianapolis, Becky talked to her dad about going to a specialist in geriatrics and memory loss. He agreed. I recalled a sermon title by Bill: "After Easter, What?" and related that to "after memory loss, what?" However, Bill didn't see a memory specialist until almost a year later.

During this early stage, Bill recognized he had memory loss. On the phone with our friend Bill V. in Oregon, my Bill related how he was struggling with dementia. Bill V. encouraged us by saying my husband may have lost some brain cells, but he still had far more than most ministers have. We placed ourselves in a position to rely upon God's leading. One Sunday evening after Bible study at FLCC, Bill asked Pastor Dan not to call on him again for answers; he now recognized his memory failed him. So much had vanished. He needed to be honest with himself and others.

QUESTIONS FOR REFLECTION:

1. Our story is not your story. How did dementia start for your loved one?
2. What changes occurred almost immediately and soon increased?

Finding New Feelings and Frustrations

I didn't count my present life as happy, because the necessary changes due to Bill's condition became unpleasant. Happiness can be superficial and temporary. But my life remained full of joy. I know joy comes from the Lord and includes a focus on the bonded relationship Bill and I still had. As for happy thoughts, I made exchanges. This may sound sad, not how happiness is acquired. My deep-down joy related to following Jesus, resting in His presence, doing what pleased Bill and not self-directed during my failures. Helping him be content pleased me and honored the Lord. That attitude didn't always surface in our daily lives; life became uncertain among our trials and frustrations.

Bill's memory loss concerned us both. One night he asked me where we got our coffee table. We had bought the furniture from the shop owned by the father-in-law of our son John. I said John's wife had the same name as our daughter Becky. He couldn't get his head around John's Becky. I explained John's wife had died. He asked how she died. I answered, "Lev's Disease." He said, "Oh, I forgot. Now I remember." I didn't mean my response to insult or patronize Bill; I wanted him to know I respected him as well as loved him.

One day he left to attend a pastors prayer meeting, but soon returned frustrated. He forgot the street name and couldn't find the new church location. Bill exhibited some depression due to his memory loss and inability to serve as he had for years. To keep mentally sane, we both had to fight off discouragement.

On our way home from the church's Thanksgiving service, Bill talked about not using his computer anymore. It was because he had difficulty getting a new program to work. He had earlier given me his debit card, saying he couldn't be trusted, forgetting what he'd charged. I was fearful about where this would lead—the unknown of Bill's memory loss. We questioned things present and things to come as we anticipated the unknown. Bill needed confirmation that Christ is never disconnected from us. We have His peace.

Added to his acknowledgement of memory loss, Bill began to berate himself. His conversations tended to turn into who's right or wrong. He would say, "I don't have a brain anymore" or

"I'm stupid" or "I'm dumb." It became difficult to reorient his spirits, and sadness would envelop me. I asked God to calm me and give me a tone of acceptance, to uphold Bill and not be critical. He did that enough on his own.

Doctors Visits

I accompanied Bill for his six-month check-up with our primary care physician. He gave a referral to a neurologist regarding Bill's memory loss. Because I needed to fill holes in his memory, I sat in on all Bill's check-ups. In February Bill had his first visit with the neurologist who prescribed two brain scans. Results from Bill's CT scan came back normal. During the follow-up visit, Bill could not answer questions from the nurses, and he looked at me. I supplied needed clarification, not comfortable with my new role. Twice he asked the PA the same question and twice she answered him graciously.

At home most mornings a sweet songbird outside greeted me with her chirping. One day in March I relished her greeting, as we were scheduled for Bill's EEG test and follow-up appointment with the neurologist. Our visit had its good and questioning results. Test results eliminated many possibilities about the cause of Bill's memory loss.

The doctor reported the memory loss was not caused by the oxygen depletion or sedative during his hospital stay for Legionnaire's disease. Tests showed the oxygen supply in his brain was good. However, other areas of concern appeared. The neurologist diagnosed hardening of the arteries as the cause of Bill's dementia. Reasonable, but not solely what I suspected. On doctor's orders, I requested a supplement from a mail-order pharmacy. We scheduled a follow-up appointment in June, with hope of a path to follow.

Bill's prescribed medications were meant to slow down the process, not to cure. The progression of the disease is, of course, a decline. This early stage of dementia progressed slowly, but did not last the longest. Some days it seemed we saw improvement, but eventually we revisited the same issue. The next day or next hour revealed repetition of a symptom or new symptoms appeared.

Finances

During this period we had issues about finances, not how much we had in the bank or investments, but how we spent our income. Bill asked whether he should get a part-time job. He mainly wanted money to give away. Such as, he bought a laptop computer for a visitor from Germany, and that was fine. He also helped a woman who needed employment. I often went along with his temperament of being generous, but we didn't agree about what enables a person's weakness.

Bill got hooked on ordering from Publishers Clearing House (PCH). He agreed he should stop, but didn't. Perhaps my attitude was wrong about Bill's orders; I too did not always spend money wisely. We are not the sole owners of our income. Bill's motivation to make PCH orders was associated with his anticipation of winning the sweepstakes. My objections to his online connection with PCH had to do with the unneeded items he would purchase. By the time he quit, he'd spent over $600 on needless stuff. I told Bill that if he won, I'd eat a lot of crow.

The date of the PCH contest closed. Not pleasant; we'd been disagreeable during the whole process. A few months later Bill asked for his email address. I saw PCH as it appeared on his computer screen. Taking our son's advice, I told Bill he could not order anything and why. He quietly turned off his computer. That worked.

Bill's Driving

Bill has always been a safe driver, and yet my anxiety increased when he steered too close to a vehicle or didn't see direction signs. He listened quietly as I expressed my fear.

In January of 2012 we left an Emmaus Gathering at a Terre Haute church and a sheet of ice covered the parking lot, with roads slick with ice. Driving home was a nightmare—slow traveling complicated by hilly areas. We arrived home, but not quite. We couldn't get up the driveway. I apologized for all my fretting, nervousness, and fear throughout our trip home. Bill's understanding of road conditions made him a wise driver.

One Sunday morning we were met with new snow, but Bill drove his 4WD truck and we made it to church safely. On the way home, Bill spouted impatient comments, berating other drivers and how they didn't act responsibly. Hearing these accusations, I cringed and reacted negatively.

We later had a brief but productive talk about how I continued to be critical of his driving. I was fearful of having an accident and getting severely injured. Although I was critical of his driving, he'd been an accident-free driver most of his life. We both needed to work on attitude, actions, and reactions.

One Sunday on our way to church, Bill and I argued about his approach at one traffic light. He turned left on a red light and said it was alright since no cars were in sight. Going against the light made sense to him, but he had made a law unto himself. After consulting a friend, a deputy sheriff, I told Bill he had been wrong about the law.

One night Bill acted confused as he drove from a Wycliffe benefit dinner. He didn't recognize the lane to our home. Turning into Reese's Corner, a gas station past our house, we parked and I took over driving home. After writing the children, they responded that their dad's reasoning power was diminishing. I agreed. Bill's abilities declined faster than I'd hoped.

Bill could no longer drive—a direct order from both the State Police and our family doctor. The conversation with the police was initiated by Becky, following an incident while I had surgery in a hospital in Indianapolis. The Saturday night after my back surgery, Bill stayed at the Gearharts' home. He informed our daughter he needed to go back to Terre Haute to get appropriate clothes to wear at church. He only had blue jeans with him, my fault about not checking what he packed. Becky told her dad it was too late to go home and their church wouldn't object to his wearing jeans.

The next morning as Paul got ready for church to lead the youth class, he noticed our car wasn't there. He alerted Becky, and she phoned her three brothers to report their dad had left. Not knowing where he had driven or if he could find our home by himself, she phoned the police to report her dad missing. She also called Pastor Dan W.

in Terre Haute, asking him to go to our house, to check if her dad had arrived there.

After two trips, Dan found Bill at home, along with the local police. Bill changed clothes and went to church with Dan who phoned Becky. After calling her brothers, she drove to Terre Haute and waited outside the church for service to end. Meeting her dad at the back of the church, she told him they were going to her house after getting more clothes for him. She took our car keys and left our car at our house.

When Becky reported to the Indianapolis police that she found her dad, the police strongly advised he should not be driving, asking her twice if she understood. "Yes," she replied, satisfied they made a good decision. Later our doctor also gave the same order.

Houses For Sale

Since we could no longer keep up the maintenance on our property, we decided to downsize our home, including four bedrooms on twelve acres of land. Bill's dementia and my health continued downhill. Contacting a local realtor, we put a For Sale sign in the front lot and started looking for a smaller house. This process took two years as we found it difficult to grasp a move off our land. We looked at several houses, but none suited us.

Bill indicated he did not want to move, and we took down the For Sale sign and declined an offer.

Becky called to encourage us to move to Indianapolis as she expressed concern for us. Unsure of such a move away from all that's familiar, we promised Becky we'd ask for God's wise choices. Brenda D., Indianapolis realtor, showed us four houses for sale. Bill, however, liked the one that would not be downsizing.

Making a trip to Indianapolis, we viewed one house on the block where Becky and Paul lived. Surely more convenient, but it rained hard that day and the basement had water in it. We voted that one out and saw others. Becky's son Stephen told his mom, "Granny wants to downsize more than Grandpa does."

To live near Becky would be good, but quite a change. We needed to trust God to provide our needs. Moving away from what was familiar and where people respected Bill proved the main crux. Desiring unity, I needed Bill to agree on when, where, and why. The pressure was off me; God's wisdom should rule. A more efficient home would suit our declining physical and mental health, a place where we would receive help along with opportunities to keep the ministries God entrusted to us.

Not yet knowing where to move, we started to prepare our house for sale. Becky and Paul came to help. Paul power-washed all the brick, and Becky saw to improvements indoors. With the For Sale sign posted up front again, we added tasks in preparation to move: de-cluttering, sorting, packing, painting, and repairing.

I asked our children and grandkids to indicate what they wanted. Some requested furniture items, and we were glad to honor their requests. As King Solomon declared: there is "a time to keep and a time to throw away" (Ecclesiastes 3:6b). Decluttering as we downsized made me evaluate what's important. The snare remained about house, land, books, things. Sadly my heart held tightly to our possessions.

Cheryl R., our Terre Haute realtor, came to take photos of our house and property, needing specs in preparation to put it on the market. While my mind understood this was right, my heart stayed at home. When referring to the sale, I called it a house; I would be "at home with Bill," wherever that might be. As Cheryl and Bill walked around the property, a sale seemed final but not sad. Long ago I had placed our home in God's hands, and soon He would direct us elsewhere.

We viewed houses in Indianapolis, but none said, *this is it*. Navigating around heavy traffic made us want to stay where it seemed safer. A few days later I phoned Becky to report, "We are not moving to Indy. We are comfortable here." Then Bill surprised me by saying, "If we're going to move, we need to do it." That was affirmation. He added, "I don't want to move to Indy *unless* we find a house really close to Becky, like next door." So the process continued a step closer toward Indianapolis.

While in Indianapolis looking at houses, our Terre Haute realtor showed our house to a particular couple, the same who expressed interest in our house when we had it for sale 18 months earlier. A few days later they made an offer and requested a survey of the property.

Our house sold. Wow! Now what? We set June 30, 2017 for closing with possession two weeks later. We had to find a house, pack, clean, and move out. I kept looking at what I'd miss: the room where I read and wrote, the green countertop in the kitchen, but most of all the beautiful views out every window—the woods and a Narnia lamp on a trail. It seemed like turning a fact of existence into an act of faith.

Becky wrote an email to express her thoughts. I printed it to read off-screen and cried through most of it. Being open and caring, she identified my fears about moving to Indianapolis. Our move would be best for the present and future, but dealing with upcoming changes still haunted me. With renewed conviction I recited: "Forget the former things; do not dwell on the past. See I am doing a new thing" (Isaiah 43:18). The "new thing" proved to be a struggle.

Remember Bill said: "I don't want to move to Indy *unless* we found a house really close to Becky." Reporting that to her, she and Paul began looking at houses designed with "mother-in-law quarters." Bill and I went to Indy and viewed two possible houses. One did not have privacy to accommodate Becky's son, Stephen, and his wife, Emily, who planned to live with us while finishing his doctorate at Indiana State University. The other house had privacy for all of us and was located closer to their church.

We made an offer on the second house, and the owners accepted. We set July 5, 2017 as the closing date. Neither the Gearharts nor we had trouble selling our houses. We worked through the finances, purchasing this house without a mortgage. A first for both of us.

Because our son John had recently retired as an air traffic controller, he gave time to come pack our needed belongings, and to distribute items we had no room to keep. When John asked about an item, whether to keep, give away, or put it in an auction, I recited its history. John finally asked, "Can you answer in less than 24 words?" A teaser, but it worked.

Books were the hardest to give away, especially those in Bill's library. Ministry books went to Bill Jr., our oldest son who pastors a church in Ohio. Other books we gave to pastors and friends who taught homeschool; but many we sent to either Good Will or the Salvation Army. John also rented a U-Haul to take furniture to his son Tommy in Louisville where he had a new job. The house began to look empty, yet packed boxes filled many areas.

Bill Jr. and Rhonda arrived for a week, along with their daughter Anna and family to attend a conference in Indianapolis. They received their requested items. Our move meant quite an adjustment in space—going from a house we owned with four bedrooms and 12 acres to what amounted to an apartment with a living room, study, bedroom, and bath. Was I to accept what we would leave behind and adjust willingly toward what lay ahead?

Home in Indianapolis

On July 16, 2017 with a moving van and helpful friends, we headed to our new address in Indianapolis. I soon called our downsized apartment the East Wing because the sun woke us up. We had a home filled with three generations: Bill and me, Becky and Paul, and Stephen and Emily. We shared the kitchen and dining room with good conversations around the table, and the family room where we watched TV together many evenings. We started attending Southport Presbyterian Church, our choice because Paul and Becky have active ministries there.

We set up a bank account with a credit union. Becky and I got our drivers' licenses, and Bill got only a photo ID, a decision on which the family united. The clerk explained that Bill surrendered his privileges to drive but still had freedom to vote in elections. Hearing this as if the first time, Bill glared at me briefly but signed the form. It must have been humiliating. A friend once told me: "My choices affect others, especially those I love." This proved a dramatic change with me as the sole driver. Was I ready?

Bill asked one afternoon if we bought this house. "Yes, we and the Gearharts." Then he compared our share of rooms with theirs, especially their bedroom and bath. He had lost so much—our house, land, and friends in Terre Haute. But in the exchange, we owned a home and received needed help.

One day Paul asked me if this experiment was going well with us. I replied, "This is not an experiment; it's a commitment." Two added advantages: our daughter is a nurse and her husband quite the handyman around the house. Both are also compassionate. Our move opened a new chapter in our lives, leaving friends and work we had known for over 28 years. In the study room shared with Bill, we each worked or played at our computers on separate desks positioned at opposite walls.

When we first came to live with Becky and Paul, she gleaned from reading about dementia patients who often don't remember when to eat. She placed a bowl of snacks on the kitchen counter for her dad. This may help some people with dementia. However, Bill loved his food, and reminded us when it was time to eat.

Shortly after we moved to Indianapolis Bill had his first doctor's appointment. We set a time for Bill to see a new neurologist who gave the diagnosis of Alzheimer's disease. The doctor also asked him some questions and had him perform a few balance exercises. Upon returning from that visit, Bill asked why he was there and what the doctor did for him. I explained that the doctor dealt with his memory loss and renewed his prescriptions. Bill said the doctor didn't talk with him. Perhaps Bill noticed most conversations happened between the doctor, Becky, and me. I repeated to Bill some questions the doctor asked, the answers Bill gave, and to what he could not respond. Bill did not recall any of that. With no memory of what went on in the doctor's office, he moved away from me. What he didn't remember didn't happen. This lack of memory revealed the neurologist's diagnosis.

In August of 2017 we celebrated our 60th wedding anniversary with a picnic. Family from other states gathered at a nearby park where we feasted and caught up with members we don't see often. During our 60 years together we've experienced more joy than grief. Our days have been filled with love, with or without expression. Our marriage has been one of covenant-keeping love. Through our whole married life, we remained faithful to each other.

Without hesitation I could testify Bill has been the greatest living influence in my life. What has he taught me? His preaching has had a big impact on my spiritual growth. Bill believed the Bible to be *the* truth, the light and guide for daily living. He has also lived it. Perhaps people recalled more his emphasis on rules and regulations, and not known his mercy. Along with others, I valued his conduct as not having any pretense.

With dementia, Bill's condition became a balancing act. One day he would be pleasant and chipper, saying, "I like you." Another day, he greeted the morning and me with a stare, a non-verbal expression which worried me a short while. Sometimes he didn't answer my questions. Then finally he spoke. Was he being stubborn? If so, why? The disease often showed itself in disturbing ways.

I grew tired of Bill asking me the same questions over and over—such as, when are we eating?

And his facial expressions made him look absent. Tired of it all, I was still glad he was present and would not want it any other way. Yes, I preferred his former self—that intellectual, confident person—before dementia. But it was wishful thinking, and couldn't be realized. The problem and solution were both mine in acceptance. Stay sweet. Be kind.

Becky decided it would be good if the family got a dog. This decision related especially to her dad, believing it would bring him pleasure. He did like holding the puppy as we watched TV in the evenings. Purchased from a rescue center, Juliet (or Jules as we called her) was part Beagle and Labrador with soft brown fur and silky ears. Her eyes even looked like she wore eyeliner. Before long she received a lot of attention from Bill and would come to his desk when she wanted to go outside. That had added advantages of getting Bill out of his chair and giving him a job.

Questions for Reflection:

1. When and how did family members get involved in care?
2. Relate your doctors' visits and how they were helpful.
3. Was there a major decision, such as moving or adding another caregiver?

Fear vs. Faith

During the progression of Bill's dementia I discovered the best and worst in me. While facing my fears, my faith stayed grounded in Christ. Nothing could separate me from God's presence: neither my fears of today nor my worries about our tomorrows. Christ helped me know my identity and what I could manage well. Created on purpose and for a purpose, I tried to align myself with God's will.

Years ago while a professor at Asbury College, Bill's season of depression affected his self-confidence. Now along with his memory loss, he exhibited a measure of depression. Before God, Bill and I had made a binding covenant. I continued to keep my vow as a loving wife, now adding to be his caregiver. Granted, because of his mental decline, our relationship became different, but still based on love and faithful commitment to our marriage vows.

Victory rested first in my mental capacity. Hardest to conquer became my emotional state, an attitude problem. With Bill, my poor attitude often surfaced. I needed to adopt a better mental acceptance of his condition. Too often when insisting on my routine, one could hear a selfish tone in my voice. My treatment of Bill shifted daily and within a day, and pride surfaced in how I reacted. Disappointment set in, leading me to ask forgiveness from God and Bill.

Married to a wonderful, affectionate man, I rejoiced to have him by my side. He threw me kisses, held my hand, and frequently said he loved me. He walked in a marching fashion, and often slapped his thighs like beating a drum. All of that I found enjoyable.

For what could I be hopeful? I hoped Bill's dementia progressed slowly; medical science has determined it would not go away nor would healing of this disease be available soon. I hoped he continued to enjoy life. And as long as I stayed able—physically and emotionally—I'd care for him until the end (his or my death). Wanting to deal kindly and efficiently, I prayed to be adequate into our future. A quote, attributed to Robert Louis Stevenson, "Make the most of the best and the least of the worse," was on my mind. But I didn't always face a problem in such a manner. I expected too much from Bill and gave too little grace for myself.

Admittedly, we had an advantage: Becky was our resident nurse with her knowledge of medications and their function. Responding to her dad's approaching incontinent accidents, she understood no medication could cure the condition.

Aleen P., care coordinator at church, gave good advice about Bill's issues. Aleen gleaned from her work in a care facility and contacts with church members who needed someone to listen. She offered suggestions about Bill's lack of cleanliness and his problem with increasing incontinence. Our church had family restrooms which Bill and I could use together, allowing me to clean up after him.

One night, in the early stage, Bill went to the bathroom, and returned to the bedroom to ask, "Do we do this in the morning or now?" He referred to taking a shower. He did not often use exact words, but gave hand motions. This routine changed before long.

Totally confused one morning, Bill needed to be shown where we stored items in the kitchen. We began a new routine of eating breakfast together. The next morning, Bill prepared the coffee and his cereal. That process would also change.

Habits and Helping

Bill's daily habits included looking through the news online and then playing computer solitaire and minesweeper. Most days he read the devotional publication mailed from our former church. It's the only thing he read, so reminding him became important.

Forgetfulness often upset us both. He looked at the cards on the computer screen and asked how to play the solitaire game he'd chosen. Since I didn't know, Becky helped him. A little time passed and he played the game by himself.

Ways of "helping" involved change. Moving to Indianapolis, Bill assumed several jobs around the house. At first he helped Paul mow the lawn, but soon Bill's energy and ability to do the task gave out. He later watched from our study window while Paul mowed. On days when the grass needed attention, Bill asked if he could mow, but I convinced him Paul would get to it.

As exercise, Bill walked around the block, about a mile. At first, I walked with him, but due to my arthritis I soon quit, confident he knew the way. Bill would leave out the front door and turn left at the sidewalk, returning from the right. One day he reported he had seen new houses. I discovered he had started from the right to walk around the block. Thus, houses looked different from that perspective. If he met neighbors, he greeted them with a smile.

Bill eagerly took to washing dishes after meals. Our grandson's wife, Emily, said, "Grandpa is the best dishwasher I know." Bill continued to assume his self-appointed job, and he stacked plates at the table, ready to start his job. But this changed. I yelled, "Use soap!" while Bill stood at the sink. These became the most repeated words in the kitchen.

Caregivers might wonder: Why would using soap to wash dishes be such a point of resistance? It's fundamental—the ability to reason diminishes when the brain is not working properly. As dementia progresses, certain nerve connections in the brain are interrupted, and these connections become blocked.

The scene at the sink was oft repeated and could get intense. After saying, "use soap," I'd put soap on his sponge and then he might say he already used soap. I did not see it, so I said, "Either you use soap, or I wash!" Bill continued the process, or he stepped away and quit. Unpredictable and unpleasant. I dried items left in the dish drainer, but my sour attitude showed.

Some of his habits at the sink were not to our liking—rinsing all the dishes thoroughly before washing them, running hot water on full blast during the whole process, wiping all the sinks dry (even during meal preparation), and placing the dishcloth between sinks where it would be in the way. But even after expressing our preferences, he continued to perform these his way.

Should not Bill agree to change, to act as I requested over and over? As his caregiver it's up to me to adjust and not expect my husband to change. Why wouldn't he give in and allow our daughter or me to wash the dishes? Simply put, he wanted a job.

Bill had what I called "aversion to soap." He ran very hot water over the dishes and said they were clean. If we called attention to the fact he wasn't using soap, he showed me the "clean" dish. Becky started filling the sink with soapy water and putting the dishes in before her dad interacted. We didn't want to take his job away, but that's what we had to do. He also didn't like to be told, "Wash your hands." He asked why, then did it. I think he did bathe with soap, but I was not certain.

Only for a short while we allowed him to dry the dishes. We were not sure if his hands were clean, which became a big concern. He looked at the items in the dish drainer and wanted to dry them or put them away. Becky or I said they would dry on their own.

While this didn't satisfy him, we directed his attention elsewhere. I began saying, "Let's brush our teeth," and he followed me out of the kitchen. It had been a long process—from Grandpa being the "best dishwasher" and then directing him away from the sink so he would not touch the dishes. His objective was meant to be helpful; ours to keep sanitation prominent, especially in the kitchen and bathroom.

All of this pointed to Bill being job-focused. He wanted to help in the kitchen, in addition to getting and distributing mail from the mailbox. In his prayers at the table and at bedtime, Bill talked with God about what he could do. He wanted jobs. He thrived on helping his family. That's who Bill was. As a caregiver, perhaps your loved one reacts in a similar way. Although it may be difficult to find jobs, we continued to try things Bill could do. Always ready to help, Bill endured our changes with his jobs around the house. With each meal we told him again the dishes will dry without his help, at the same time guarding the dishtowel.

Food and Meals

Bill displayed a fixation on eating. This didn't make it easy to follow the unwritten rule: let him do what he wants. He pointed to the clock, as if asking what I'd do about it. His hunger for food and wanting it on time (mostly due to boredom) showed this interest hadn't decreased. He often helped himself to large portions on his plate at supper, even before we offered the blessing. He gained weight, but so did I. Our usual evening treat was ice-cream, but I didn't offer it every night and dished fewer scoops.

Some funny incidents happened at the table with Bill's food, even before we sat down to eat. At one supper meal Becky served a bowl of leftover pot roast with potatoes and carrots. When Bill came to the table, he placed crunchy wheat crackers over the top of his stew. After I took them off, he put them back. Satisfied, he ate it his way.

Bill had a good appetite. In fact, the only problem depended on our not getting meals ready early enough for the clock in his stomach. At noon on the dot he turned his chair around from his computer desk, stomped his feet to get my attention, as he pointed to the wall clock. I'd say, "We'll eat in half an hour." This didn't please him. One evening meal was later than usual and it made Bill so angry he sat at the table but refused to eat. My only recourse was not to serve ice cream later as we watched TV.

Changing my time schedule would delight him, but not considered by me a reasonable time frame between meals. His attitude affected me, but not to the degree of getting his way. I'm the one who needed to change, because getting his own meals would pose a problem.

Bill devoured peppermints by the gallon. Yes, we buy them in gallon tubs, the soft kind because he chewed them. Telling Bill the dentist said the hard mints were not good on his teeth, his response was, "What does he know?" Of course, sugar intake was also not good. One day Bill said pathetically, "I have a problem," as he showed me the empty dish for his peppermints.

And speaking of teeth, Bill acquired a new upper denture which had not been to his liking. Perhaps it didn't fit properly. A few days later while holding his denture, he asked me where "this" came from, adding, "I don't like." After offering to bring him for an adjustment, he said no. He often took out his denture at the table to lick it and to pick food from it. We had decided on a new one, because he had broken two teeth and glued them in his 12-year-old denture. I stored that one; and the costly new denture was better.

At the dinner table, Bill seemed to be in his own little world, and it's unknown what he was thinking. We even talked about him and no recognition showed on his face. One, because of his hearing loss, and two, he was disinterested. He could not follow the conversation. If we asked him a question, we interrupted his world and no conversation started. I wanted his attention, to be involved with me and our family. What was different? During previous times at the table, Bill would have been the one who started and maintained the topic of conversation.

When confronted with options, Bill could not choose. Preparing our lunch, I might ask, "Sandwiches or soup?" He generally said, "Whatever you want." One Saturday around noon as we left the post office, I gave Bill the option to stop by McDonald's for lunch. He said, "Whatever you want." Did he want to eat inside or take it home? His answer again, "Whatever you want." Why doesn't his agreement please me? It's not his usual mannerism.

Since Becky was the better cook, she planned and prepared our evening meals—what we ate and when. If the clock showed 6 PM, Bill asked, "Are we going to eat?" I said, "Well, yes." His retort, "Tomorrow?" Me: "Yes, we'll eat tomorrow and today." My response indicated an arrogant manner, perhaps to exasperate him. While the mental part of me recognized his demands as part of the disease, the emotional part of me wanted to fight against this unwanted disease. Instead, this retaliation became an arrogant attack on the one I loved in the vain hope this may turn back the clock. The fact is, no one has survived Alzheimer's disease.

Bill often went into the kitchen to see what Becky was cooking. She may be preparing a meal or working on her bake shop menu. Selling her baked goods added concern about Bill being inconsistent with cleanliness. Although he wanted to help, Becky would not engage him in her process. Instead, she would ask him to set the table. "How many?" "Four." "Which dishes?" "You decide." "What do we need?" "Forks and knives." He may know the difference. Then he might stand near the counter and watch her, wanting to grab something to wash before dinner. Eventually I would come to the kitchen and redirect Bill's attention or lead him to our rooms.

At One's Core

On the positive side in this stage of dementia, Bill rarely got upset with us. His temper usually was in response with my correcting him, such as not using soap. Our son John gave fresh meaning to this. When someone is drunk, that person exhibits the core of his personality. If he's kind, he will be a kind drunk. If he's an angry person, he will be an angry drunk. His dad was not an angry person, nor did he get drunk. At the core, his dad was an authoritative person, and didn't take well to being corrected or told what to do or not to do. Thankfully, Bill's forgetfulness meant his discontent didn't last long.

To this core of being an authoritarian, add Bill's character trait of integrity. I've often said Bill's middle name could be integrity. He taught, preached, and lived the truth. His ministry and life showed dedication to the truth. Thus, if corrected, he associated that with what he knew as valid and true.

During the coronavirus pandemic, Bill didn't understand the new restrictions. All those weeks we could not attend church, he asked why. We explained, but of course, he would forget. We explained again the next week. Returning to attend church, we wore masks for four Sundays. Only the first time did Bill protest; and then wore it without questioning. However, he asked why everyone else wore masks.

Bill verbally expressed his love, more often than before this disease. As we kissed good night, he said, "I love you too." Most every morning he hugged me with, "I love you." A new and welcome trait. A card he sent me years ago read: "You've always been so much better than I am at expressing your love, but over the years you've tolerated my inadequacy and the many times I have presumed on your tolerance." In former years he expressed himself openly more often in writing than in spoken words. Now he spoke of his love with the few words he still knew.

Love that's silent can become weak. Throughout our years of marriage, Bill taught me how to be open and to express my love. Now both in his table blessings and night prayers, he centered on thankfulness. He repeated the same words, but at least he verbally offered thanks.

He smiled a lot and was generally happy. He had the habit of watching TV alone in late afternoons (westerns or comedies), because he got bored with computer games. Together we watched TV after supper, and Bill wanted me there by his side. He even watched me brush my teeth and led me to the family room. Bill often dozed during a movie, but he was more attentive to comedies. I should do better about selecting what we watched.

One change bothered me, but it's not unusual with dementia. Bill exhibited what's called startling episodes. In the middle of the night he flailed his arms around and called out one word like "Oh" or "Ma," and sometimes he grabbed my arm. To comfort him, I touched his shoulder and repeated, "It's alright." No idea what he'd been dreaming. These episodes happened also when he dozed while watching TV, although he wouldn't admit it. In a moment he became comfortable again and forgot the episode. Once or twice a week these occurred, night or day.

During this journey we were refreshed continually like a spring that never ran dry. In the ordinary God worked out what He was working in me. Although grateful for a sense of rhythm in our lives, some routines changed with time. Such as, we quit allowing Bill to walk around the block by himself; he would more likely lose his direction on the return route.

The emphasis grew in how the disease affected Bill's daily life and mine. As his wife and primary caregiver, too often I became irritable, angry, or sad due to constant changes. Also I had to take the lead. Finding my voice after all those years was not easy, because Bill had been the spokesman in our household. Besides, his answers rang true. Now I spoke for him, answering questions directed toward him during Sunday school at church.

Resources

Through books and articles about Alzheimer's and dementia in general, Becky and I gained a layperson's knowledge of how it functions and what to expect. Each book conveyed good advice and perspective on Bill's condition. *New Every Day* by Dave Meurer provided us with the expression we repeated frequently. We could not judge one day by another. How Bill acted one day didn't mean it would be the same way later in the day or several days later. Each day was new. We could not predict what the next day would bring by what we saw today or yesterday or even last week. The phrase "new every day" continued to be true. Each day was new and without concrete expectations. The disease operated that way.

Second Forgetting by Dr. Benjamin Mast encouraged me to remember God does not forget. He loves us. Even with these challenges, God extends grace to both patient and caregiver. Memory loss is the major problem, but dementia affects other functions, even motor skills. Our former primary care physician informed us Alzheimer's disease is not actually a cause of death. It does, however, lead to the cause such as a patient forgetting to swallow or even to breathe.

Pauline Boss, in her book *Loving Someone Who Has Dementia,* introduced the term "ambiguous loss," meaning someone with dementia is both present and away. Bill was still Bill but not what he used to be. That fact involved grief of an unusual dimension for a loved one, a loss of who they once were. Loss affected both patient and caregivers. We were here but he was not. We cared for Bill at a distance no matter how close we were.

Charles R. Swindoll once wrote, "Life is 10 percent what happens to us and 90 percent how we react to it." Some areas in myself were not pretty. What was hidden deep in my psyche surprised me, triggering some unpleasant responses. Unfortunately, it was unlikely that any change would happen rapidly.

Affirmations

One afternoon on the way home from our dental appointments, I wanted Bill to know his hygienist told me he's sweet. Bill tried to repeat what I'd said, but he didn't get the word right, instead saying "tweet." Finally he said "sweet," but nothing more; his understanding was faulty. My goal—that Bill be encouraged—didn't register. I tried to dismiss it, but I was disappointed Bill didn't find the communication positive.

My wanting Bill to be better wasn't realistic. Accepting what this disease brought to him, to me, and to our family grew into a difficult learning process over a long period of time. It's not what we desired for him or us, yet we had no power to change it. We couldn't say, "It's all better now," as though treating a child who got a minor scrape on a knee.

Consider childish behavior. In some ways, Bill acted like a child who wanted his way, while I acted like a parent who believed my way was the best. He reacted strongly to negatives like "stop" and "don't." If I treated him like a child, correcting his actions and explaining in simple language, he gave up on himself. How must I react to this strong urge? Needing peace as we advanced into our uncertain future, God was able to keep us strong even through what had been lost.

Words Bill heard did not always compute with their meanings, whether it's "rinse" when we're at the sink or "blanket" when making up the bed. While putting fresh sheets on our bed, Bill came to help. Asking him to get the white blanket, he put his pillow on the bed. Taking it off, and in a scolding tone, I said, "That's a pillow. Here is the white blanket." He did not understand my words or why I got upset.

On some occasions Bill stood firm with what suited him in the moment. For example, what he wore to church. He picked out his clothes and asked if they're okay. If I suggested a sweater vest, he wanted to pick out the color, usually blue, the one he wore the past several Sundays. There's no changing his mind. Well, he did make a choice.

Before time to leave anyplace, I must tell Bill about five minutes earlier than actual time. He could be fixated on something else, such as whether to take his Bible, which he didn't open. Here's the man who always got me and our kids to church or any event way before starting time. Now I'm the one pushing for us to be on time.

About his Bible, he quit reading it. On occasion I suggested he take out his Bible to read. One morning he asked me where it's stored and what he's supposed to do with it. His usual answer back to me: "I've already read it." The truth: he lost comprehension of written material. We first noticed this during an eye exam. He saw the letters but couldn't identify them.

Again, this both frustrated and made me sad. As a pastor, Bill was studious. He understood the biblical languages and had taught those in college. He did extensive research when preparing every message. Now he didn't want to read his Bible for his own benefit. Not the real reason; he hid the fact that reading became a chore. He wasn't able to do it. Not accepting this, I tried often to persuade him to read. That's saying something about myself, because I wasn't ready to face reality, the drastic changes in Bill's desires and abilities.

The biggest change (it seemed to me) was how dementia robbed Bill of his identity, who he had been. Although I wanted my husband before dementia, I still loved this man I've known most of my life. Outside of an unknown cure, change won't happen. Living as a caregiver can be arduous *or* it can be a learning process, even including joy.

Questions for Reflection:

1. Have you had to deal with food issues?
   Too much or too little? Or fussy?
2. What habits or chores had to change?
   Because of cleanliness or keeping order?
3. How would you describe the core of your
   loved one and how did personality change?

PART II

The Messy Middle— How It Continued

I have been consistent with journaling, and most reports of this memoir first appeared in my journals between 2010 and 2025. The following dated entries show a variety of subjects.

5-10-19—Some episodes caused me to wonder if a change was permanent. We went to Terre Haute to attend the hooding ceremony of our grandson Stephen's doctoral degree in physical therapy. Paul drove with Bill up front; Becky and I sat in the back. We arrived at Hulman Center, and Bill got out of the van, unstable with his gait. He said, "Whatever is blowing, turn it off." He referred to the air conditioner being on during the trip, but he had said nothing while in the car.

He was cold and shivering, so Paul handed his own jacket to Bill. We helped him into the building and entered the section for our seats. An attendant, noticing Bill's condition, pointed us to chairs suitable for the disabled, behind fiberglass and on a level where we would not have to go down an aisle of steps.

Becky, a few rows down from the partition, needed to save seats and requested a text about any problem with her dad. Paul brought Bill some snacks. We noticed Bill's hands and lips had turned blue, so Paul reported to Becky. She asked an usher to send an EMT as she headed our way. The team checked Bill's blood pressure and pulse. The BP reading registered higher than usual. They asked about medications and if he were diabetic.

With no indications of serious problems, I signed a paper as POA (Power of Attorney). Bill warmed up, ate a snack, but showed little response during the graduation exercises. We attended the dessert reception, with Bill still a bit unstable even after we stopped at Applebee's for a late supper. The next day Bill didn't recall anything about the graduation or his episode. I decided I'd need to keep his health and medication record in my purse at all times.

Sky Gazer

Leaving church, Bill looked at the clouds, commenting how grey they were, and rainy weather soon to come. When looking out our study window, he noticed the cloud coverage and made predictions on the weather.

5-21-19—As a sky gazer, Bill's weather forecasts could also interrupt plans. While my sister Martha and her husband, Jimmy, visited from New Mexico (May 2019), we decided on a day trip to Conner Prairie. The colonial exhibits represented the area's past history and our walks between scenes provided some exercise.

Those exhibits of the past were not known to us sisters, but many were reminiscent of Jimmy's growing up years. He lived it and would fill in details related to the exhibit. Jimmy stood and talked with Bill, who also seemed to relate to the exhibits. Jimmy informed us about what a certain tool did then and how it had changed. We appreciated how Bill listened and interacted with Jimmy, not anything Martha or I could relate. She and I would look at the details of the exhibit, but Jimmy could examine and add to its historic meaning. That seemed to please Bill, and we were glad they had each other to share the details.

We departed earlier than planned, because Bill gazed at the sky and predicted a storm would soon come our way. He kept talking about it, so we left to ease his anxiety. However, no rain on our way home.

Martha later wrote: "The last time we visited, Bill's memory issues presented a different man than I'd known all my life. He didn't know Jimmy, but seemed to know me, which blessed me. We saw anger outbursts, and that wasn't the Bill I knew and loved. When I had wanted spiritual advice from Bill, it was evident he wasn't able to process what was needed. My grief was compounded knowing it was even tougher for Ann to walk through. To lose your mate bit by bit, absent but there. I was honored to have been in the same family."

Connecting with Family

I sent emails to family, giving updates. Two years after moving to Indianapolis (July of 2019), I wrote in an email to our sons:

"Your dad had one of his *new* days. With a blank expression on his face, he became more confused than previous days. Becky brought Dad to help with snacks for Vacation Bible School at church. He didn't understand requests, while mixing words and their meanings. We can't depend on how one day affects the next. It's the way with dementia."

Our son John replied, "In my humble opinion, you need to stop expecting things from Dad and just help him in whatever few things he needs." I didn't reply, finding it hard to agree.

A few days later I responded with an email stating:

"Your dad's progression is slow. Some days I think we may have turned a corner not to revisit, but it's not so. The next day or next hour change happens. Generally up before me, he gets dressed and goes to start the coffee and his breakfast of Cocoa Puffs. One morning he came from the kitchen to ask what he's supposed to do (not in those words).

"I'm grateful for time to be with your dad during days and nights, and I still have time to write. If Dad has become more complex, he's certainly a happy forgetful camper."

8-28-19—Becky, Paul, Bill, and I attended our son John's wedding reception in Lexington, Kentucky. On the way, we again noticed how attentive Bill appeared, watching the roads and the sky. He enjoyed the ride, even commented on the clouds, saying there were fewer at home. At the reception Bill liked the food but didn't interact much with family members. He did cooperate with posing for photos.

The next evening while watching TV, Bill dozed off, and we heard him snore. Probably tired from the previous day's trip. Becky was surprised her dad had not slept in the car as we traveled home late from Kentucky. We could go out more, not only to doctors' appointments and shopping, but ride around to view the countryside. Bill liked seeing houses with land around them, reminiscent of the house we had built on 12 acres.

8-31-19—Saturday mornings Paul took Bill to church to attend the Men's Prayer Breakfast. Paul thought it worth the time, a good outlet. When Bill's not there, the men at church on Sunday would say they missed him. One Friday night Bill kept asking what happened in the morning and should he get ready. Assuring him the alarm would go off in time, he turned over and went to sleep. He said, "I know I'm stupid." I said, "You're not stupid, you just can't remember." He wasn't upset with me, only with himself. Another Saturday morning Bill was intent on getting dressed on time, but it was after midnight. It took a while for him to calm down and return to bed. Paul asked later if Bill had trouble getting ready. I said, "Not at 12:30." Was it time to re-evaluate the effort?

9-19-19—While talking to a publisher on my flip-style cell phone, the call cut off 24 times (I counted). That gave me good-enough reason to buy a new phone. Bill accompanied me to the Sprint store, meeting Paul because he was the policy holder for our family plan. At first Bill was patient, standing and watching, but the procedure took too long. After using my debit card and signing the pad, I sat while the tech attendant transferred addresses from flip variety to android phone. I asked Bill if he wanted to sit, but instead he stood over me, asking why we were there.

Several times I informed Bill we were buying a new cell phone, but he said he didn't know why he had to be there. *That* was the problem. *He* had no reason to be present; *he* was not involved. *I* made the transaction as the one who signed papers. Having no purpose ignited Bill's angst and insecurity. Paul encouraged us to leave and he'd handle the rest. In the car Bill asked again why we were there. I answered, apologized, and changed the subject.

At home, Becky reminded me of our time at the bank, applying for a home equity loan. Bill did not need to participate, no papers to sign. Paul, Becky and I handled it all. Leaving the bank, Bill asked why they didn't ask him to sign papers. Explaining was not easy. I had POA; I'm the one who signed legal papers. Getting ready to go to the phone company, I didn't use forethought to leave Bill at home with Becky.

Bill and I were together, but with our roles reversed. I was the one who did the talking, signing papers, leading. He had been happier when he led, and I leaned on him for support. The phone encounter with Bill did not, however, turn into an argument, and I was grateful.

9-25-19—For a season of eight weeks, we attended the early traditional service at church. One following day at lunch, Bill surprised me by asking, "Why did we switch when we attend worship?" (not in those exact words). I gave the reason: "We like to hear the hymns, choir, and organ in the traditional service." He explained he liked both styles of worship music, but he missed sitting with Becky and family. So we returned to the contemporary service. Family won over hymns. It also meant being welcomed back to the 9:30 Sunday school.

Being Bored

I wouldn't allow Bill to degrade himself regarding his memory loss. One day he found a harmonica in his desk and asked why it was there. I urged him to play a tune and he agreed. It sounded pretty. I put it on top of his desk for quick access, but later he said he didn't know what to play. Perhaps he only needed encouragement. Later he took out the harmonica and played a bit, but when I remarked how nicely he played, he put it back in the case. Next time I should keep quiet.

I read Colossians, chapter three. The apostle Paul wrote about putting off the old way with all its earthly trappings to find new life with all its heavenly treasures. Clothed daily in compassion, I wanted to be nice, conquer selfish thoughts and actions, and work on a gentle attitude (v. 12). I questioned whether my actions toward Bill were "as is fitting in the Lord" (v. 18). Bill's dementia didn't dismiss my part in our agreed covenant. I had assurance Bill loved me.

When Bill got bored, I was at a loss to suggest an activity he liked. Some days he did not play many computer games, didn't want to read, and definitely would not agree to play the piano or harmonica. I followed Bill Jr.'s suggestion of playing a CD of hymns and handed Bill a hymnbook. I also found some Gaither Homecoming DVD's and we played one to watch in the afternoon. He liked to ride in the car, so more often we took a short trip to nowhere in particular.

Go, Go, Go

10-4-19—Bill liked to be on the go. One afternoon he again said, "Let's go somewhere." I asked, "Where?" Bill responded, "Anywhere." Paul gave directions to Southeastway Park. Three Ts in the roads: turn L, turn R, turn L, park is on the L. "Coming back," he said, "it's tricky: no Ts for your turns." We first drove around the park, and Bill recognized where we had the family picnic for our 60th anniversary.

Parking the car, we took a trail into the woods to a creek. The path wasn't too rugged and had nice scenery. Bill looked happy I found the way back to the car and to home. My not getting lost became quite an achievement. I took photos in the park and posted one of Bill on Facebook, which received 114 likes and 30 comments.

10-21-19—I thank God that He helped me drive to and from the Hymn Sing last night. I was not sure of the alternate route because of construction. We enjoyed the singing and the meditation. Bill sang, even during the specials. Whenever words appeared on the overhead screen, he sang whether it meant the congregation or solos. On the way home, I asked if he liked the Hymn Sing. He said, "It was okay, not bad." I'd gotten used to his overall compliment—"okay"—whether for food, movies, or music.

Bill moved a step down in memory. He did not anticipate a natural physical function. While standing in front of the sink, he had no sense of needing to urinate and thus wet his clothes. Unaware of this urge, it puzzled him. After telling me what happened, Bill went to change his clothes. Before we went anywhere and several times during the day, I started suggesting to Bill that he use the bathroom.

Four o'clock one afternoon Bill turned around in his chair and said, "Let's go somewhere!" I asked where, but he had no destination in mind, what to do or see. He was bored. Becky suggested we drive to Acton, a small nearby town. We took to the road, but didn't see the downtown, only homes along Acton Road. We passed a church and Bill said we'd been there before (more of his skewed memory). I got lost only once by taking a street leading to a dead end. Soon we found the familiar Southport Road for our return trip home, stopping at Kroger to buy ice-cream.

Around 10 o'clock one morning, Bill asked if we were going anywhere. We had plans to eat out for pizza that night. He looked disappointed, so I said, "Why do you ask?" He'd gotten tired of playing solitaire on his computer. He wanted to do something different. I put on a CD of Andy Griffith's stories. He listened, not laughing much, but whistled and hummed to the familiar theme song.

Because Bill did not need to dress up daily as when he taught or preached, most days he wore jeans. When wearing a blue pullover, it matched his hazel eyes, and I told him so. His normal routine at day's end was to hang up his clothes in the closet. On laundry day I looked through his shirts and pants to pull out those with food stains. He rarely put any clothes in the dirty clothes hamper. Not a big chore, only an adjustment.

Holidays and Visits

11-9-19—Our granddaughter Anna and her triplets visited one weekend, and we observed how Bill played with each of the kids. Naomi snuggled up to him as he tickled her. Bill arm-wrestled with Ethan, and Levi asked to show him more of the card games to play on the computer. Great-grandpa seemed to be in his element with the triplets. What a joy to notice their interaction and love expressed together. Each child brought their great-grandpa into their worlds.

It's been three weeks now since God gave me a new outlook—one of contentment, not being irritated with Bill and his ways. It's only God, not me, not my way. I looked at Bill as valued, and my tone of voice changed. God's spirit is in my spirit. It's God alone; His work surpassed any skill I have. God's power worked in my weakness.

11-28-19—Thanksgiving Day with a good family gathering. John and Elaine came from Lexington; Wes and his three children arrived from Westfield. Before we ate the delicious meal prepared by Becky, John read "When the Frost Is on the Pumpkin" by James Witcomb Riley; Bill read Psalm 100; and Paul prayed the blessing. Bill didn't interact much, but it was evident he enjoyed having family here.

12-24-19—Christmas Eve. Chrissa and Léo arrived last evening from Texas, and they, along with Becky and Paul left today for Illinois to spend Christmas with Paul's mother and other family members. It's their first Christmas since Ruth moved out of her home into an independent living apartment. No pity party here; Bill and I would celebrate Christmas together. Bill played the piano as we sang Christmas carols. We also attended the Christmas Eve service at church. Christmas morning: Bill and I prepared our traditional omelets for breakfast. We later went to an open house, invited by a church family and we enjoyed good fellowship.

A New Decade

12-31-19—The end of a year and a decade. In the summer of 2010, Bill was in the hospital with Legionnaire's disease. I tasted and found the Lord was good (Psalm 34:8). Now we've experienced almost ten years of Bill's dementia. I faced a new year with hope as I asked the Lord to equip me with a bold stand and not to be fearful of life's unknown events.

With the quarantine restrictions due to Covid, we had difficulty explaining to Bill we could not go to church. Each Sunday meant another question from Bill and our repeated explanation. Paul showed Bill the news on his computer. Afterward, Bill came to our study and said, "This thing is not just here but around the world." Then he added, "This might be the end." I tried to point out we needed to be cautious but not fearful. Our church started streaming services available on TV with a few staff presenting music and a message. We watched at home, but not the same. No togetherness. Hopeful to have corporate worship back for Easter, but that didn't happen. When we did return to church, Bill had to be encouraged to wear a mask.

1-22-20—I bought Bill an electric razor. This decision came after one early morning he had gone to the bathroom while I was still in bed. He came to bed holding a tissue on his chin. He had shaved as usual, and he had cut his cheeks and chin so badly there was blood on his face, his nightshirt, down the cabinet by the sink, and on the rug. He told me he was going to stop shaving and grow a full beard (not in those words). I said, "No, I've bought you an electric razor, and you're going to use it." Often I had to be in the bathroom when he shaved and put the razor in his hand. This could become a habit.

Some days Bill repeated his shaving routine, perhaps dissatisfied the electric razor could give a close shave. We switched to electric for good reason. We decided he could shave as often as he wanted; it gave him something to do.

2-8-20—Last night Bill called me into the bathroom after his shower. The floor outside the tub was wet; the bathmat soaked and placed on the floor of the tub. His towel was wet and hung up. Of course, he didn't know how it happened. The only explanation was the plastic shower curtain could have been outside the tub or he had not closed the curtain while he bathed. I took care of all the wet items. Bill was upset with himself, so my main attention was to calm him.

5-24-20—I went to the kitchen this morning and found Bill at the sink. The crockpot was filled with soapy water—the unit, not the inside pot. The electric cord and plug were also in the sink. I told Bill this should not be washed. He argued it needed cleaning, and his arm stiffened on the edge of the sink. I got the crockpot out and dried it, saying it needed to stay that way. He said, "That's what some say." Becky tested it later and it still worked.

6-25-20—This evening Becky and Paul were out with friends. Before Bill and I got ready for bed, he put Jules in her crate, and he got angry when I loosed her. I said, "When you calm down, I'll tell you why." He got quiet and I explained that Jules needed to greet Becky and Paul when they returned home. I refused to argue and it worked.

I knew Bill's condition would get worse, like caring for a toddler with little reasoning power. I also knew God is already in our future, to meet us there with His adequacy. I'll be ready then.

7-15-20—Becky thought her dad would like helping in the church nursery, holding babies during the Sunday school hour. After one time, he said, "I don't want to do that again." Outings with Becky were termed "field trips," and Bill certainly liked going places. Becky took her dad to Walmart and he pushed the cart while she shopped. Bill went to the Indianapolis Zoo with Becky and her friend and baby daughter. It was a big-to-do, but Bill didn't remember agreeing to this event. After he returned, he offered no details to my questions. Becky said he liked seeing the animals.

7-27-20—Bill had another startling episode during the night and it was long. He yelled "Oh" repeatedly and flailed his arms around. I tried to sooth him and he awoke, not knowing where he was. It took me a while to go back to sleep, but not him. He had those startles about once a week—either during the night or when he dozed on the couch with the TV going. No explanation, except it's part of the disease. As Aleen said, these episodes were akin to Bill detaching himself from his body. When he walked around the block, he cooperated with his body. She said it would be good to have him help with tactile chores such as folding laundry.

This week I noticed how happy Bill was and how he loved to tease, to help, to be with me. I rejoice! He clapped his hands when it was his turn to do anything. He was attentive and cared about me.

8-25-20—Last night's dinner at Bonefish Grill with our family celebrated 63 years of our marriage. I also realized Bill was no longer what he had been, but a man with lost memory, understanding, and abilities. He had me order for him, and that worked well. He had two problems while eating. He didn't use his handkerchief for a runny nose, but instead used his hand or the napkin. Also he started to take out his denture when he finished eating. I asked him to wait until we got in the car, and he did. Perhaps my concern was more about how others see him. But I needed to face facts.

Hard Lessons to Learn

9-7-20—Troubles are meant to teach God's lessons. That reminds me of John Bunyan's *The Pilgrim's Progress* when stumbling blocks *on* the Way were to keep Christian and his friends *in* the Way. God can turn pain into praise and worry into worship. I this pray for our journey.

God knows me and my ways, the trials of each day, even when Bill turned on me after I used words that belittled him. He forgot it later, but I needed to uphold him as a man of integrity. What happened each day may not make sense, but I rested in God's plan. His ways are always best.

10-15-20—A month later Bill and I almost came to a fist fight one night in front of the sink. My changed attitude didn't last long. This was about soap. He had rinsed our ice-cream bowls and had the spoons in his hand when I noticed the sponge still in the rack. I moved the bowls from the drying rack. We were both angry, and our hands were flying along with our tongues. He left mad, spouting something I didn't understand.

11-17-20—As I proofed Bill's upcoming *Words* book, I read the testimony of his call to preach. Through Bill's example and his preaching I had heard God's truth explained. Bill came by my desk and I read two paragraphs to him. I said it was what he preached at WGC and it will be in his book. He clapped and his eyes watered. He had made a connection. However, when the box of books arrived the next month, Bill was surprised his name was on the cover. He said, "I don't remember this." I said, "You preached it. I got it ready for a book." As his messages got published, people had opportunity again to read and understand God's Word.

12-9-20—Bill got confused this afternoon. He talked with Becky about a man who wanted to help him, and the man was not Paul. While on my computer for a Zoom meeting, Bill told me he wanted to go someplace, but we had no plans. He headed to the closet to get his jacket, but I invited him to watch TV instead. Maybe his head cold triggered this confusion. That night he slept well and was calm the next morning.

For any family, time schedules change as children grow. Our infants often woke us up at two o'clock. Those feeding times were normal, even expected. When teenagers, they chose late at night as their time to unwind and talk to their parents. Now my husband asked questions when we were in bed around eleven o'clock. Bill thought it a good time to get something off his mind before turning over to sleep. But I didn't think it was a good time for discussion. We'd gone full circle with early morning and late night encounters.

1-5-21—One subject Bill often brought up at bedtime dealt with the location of our burial sites. Several years ago we prepared ahead for our funerals and burial, making necessary contacts in Terre Haute. We decided on the funeral home, picked out our caskets, and planned the memorial services. We chose and paid for plots in a local cemetery, with gravestones from a Terre Haute monument place. Now Bill asked if we ought to relocate the plots to Indianapolis. We rehearsed the pros and cons and solved nothing at that late hour.

After contacting our children for their opinions, they all agreed to keep it as arranged, mainly because none had plans to frequent the gravesite after the burial ceremony. So it was settled—until the next time Bill brought it up.

While I hate Alzheimer's disease, I'm not angry—either at God or my husband. My tone at times sounds harsh or frustrated while repeating answers to Bill's questions, because he soon forgot what I'd said. Like the time he saw an appointment added to his calendar for the next day: 3:30 PM Beltone. He wanted to know not only what that meant but where and how long it took to arrive. A moment later he added, "I know I'm dumb, but what is Beltone?" I replied, "You're not dumb; you've only forgotten about your scheduled appointment."

At his Beltone appointment, Bill had his hearing aids cleaned. When the tech left his office, I didn't catch at first what Bill did. He had an ear plug in his hand, taken from a small glass jar on the desk. He showed me the plug and put it close to his tongue. "That's not candy," I said, taking it away. With a frown, he grabbed another plug. I said, "Those are not for you." Not happy, he folded his hands in his lap.

Trips to ER

At times it wasn't easy to decipher Bill's condition, especially when he tried to explain an ailment. One day he complained twice about chest pains. The first time he described it as "different." With advice from our daughter, he took an aspirin as we headed to the ER. At the front desk I told the medical receptionist he complained of chest pain and added he had dementia. An aid escorted us directly to a room where nurses and aids began to administer various tests. A doctor later explained they could find nothing seriously wrong. After several hours we returned home late at night.

When a second episode happened, I resisted repeating the previous visit to the ER, so I was perhaps (no, definitely) wary about Bill's symptoms. Trying to describe his condition, he said his chest hurt but his throat also hurt. He began to belch, so I assumed he had heartburn and gave him an antacid tablet. Before long he said he was better, but his forehead felt hot.

Becky soon returned from catering a wedding rehearsal dinner. She took her dad's blood pressure and with her stethoscope she listened to his heart. Blood pressure registered in normal range and his heart rhythm good. He soon stated he was better. Grateful we didn't go for another ER visit, still I questioned my reaction. During the episode my voice got louder, because he wasn't wearing his hearing aids and his complaints were hard to understand.

Bill exhibited a good sense of humor, and he often enjoyed teasing me. When an unexplained bruise appeared on his hand or arm, he informed family members I had hit him. When it was noon and he was hungry, he said I didn't want to fix him lunch. When I got ready to volunteer at Southside Life Center or leave for an appointment, Bill pretended to act sad but said it was fine to go without him.

Handing Bill water to take a pill, he made a face; he's never liked water. When we reported some symptoms to his doctor, these indicated he might be dehydrated. We prepared an unsweetened fruit-flavored drink which he tolerated and usually drank without complaining. But sometimes he would bring his glass into the kitchen and pour the remaining drink down the sink.

Turning a Corner?

Some mornings I often wondered, "Is Bill turning a corner?" We had our normal routines and when he didn't follow them I would question if his course of action would permanently alter our routine. One such morning, he got out of bed before me. While in the bathroom, he had not shaved or taken his medication I'd placed on the counter.

He returned to the bathroom and I mentioned he needed to shave. This omission wasn't like him. Would he soon return to his previous routine?

12-31-20—Bill would often ask what day it was. He kept a calendar open on his desk and marked off the days, almost like ticking off time—another day passed. On that last day of 2020, Bill kept looking at his calendar, and he found no more days to mark through. When I handed him a 2021 calendar, he smiled. What changes could we expect with Bill in the new year?

Again, we couldn't predict what one day would hold, compared to what happened on a previous day. If one day Bill showed confusion about names of objects and where they belonged, it may not mean the next day would be the same or worse. His memory may seem better, even within the same day. As the subtitle of a book reads: we were "navigating Alzheimer's with grace and compassion." It was important to remind myself it was not Bill's choice to act this way; the disease controlled him. He didn't *decide* to forget or repeat or be confused. Blaming his changing behavior on him got me nowhere, and it ignored the facts. Better to blame the disease.

While friends visited, Bill retold an incident from his life story, but he gave a different ending. At first I corrected him, but Becky advised that wasn't good: "Let him tell the happy conclusion; it's his memory that's skewed." Knowing Bill had always been committed to truth, it was hard not to correct him. Generally the people to whom he related the story knew the true ending. Not to comment proved best, allowing the story to develop as he told it while I made eye contact with listeners.

His skewed memory also affected my choice of movies to watch. He'd say he already saw one when he hadn't. What did it matter? Any corrective response affected his attitude and mine. Becky helped me turn my corrective voice into one that led to her dad's cooperation, not upsetting him or me.

Friends Visit

"The sorrow of parting flows from the sweetness of love" (Bob Hostetler, *The Bard and the Bible*). When leaving Ephesus, the apostle Paul found it difficult leaving friends behind. We left friends behind in Vigo and Clay counties when we moved to Indianapolis. Some still kept in touch in various ways, such as visits and emails, and we were grateful.

One Sunday we had a surprise visit came from Zach and Christy Y. and their two girls. They got our address from friends and showed up at our house.

As missionaries in Nigeria, they had returned to Indiana to attend a sister's wedding. We had a nice visit, getting caught up on their lives. Zach expressed gratitude for Bill's teaching at church during his formative years.

Later in the same week, we received another visit from a missionary in Japan, Susan T. She and her mother Cecelia came, and we shared memories of our time in Waco, Texas, when Bill preached at their church. Those sermons became part of the book I compiled—*Let the Church Be the Church*. We had a week of visitors, including Brad M., president of Life Issues Institute, who phoned. Then we met at a nearby coffee shop.

Our most frequent guests were our friend Donna Dene E., pastor-friend Paul Z. and his wife Jan. Sometimes when Donna Dene came, we met for lunch at her choice of restaurant. Paul and Jan would visit a while and we'd all go for lunch. Paul also phoned on a regular basis to keep connected. Donna Dene and I texted regularly.

Friends from our years in Wilmore, Kentucky, now lived in Terre Haute. Aaron and Cynthia W. visited, bringing along Aaron's ukulele and sheet music so we could sing together. Silly fun. Then they treated us to lunch. But what I appreciated most were our conversations— remembrances of associations in churches and the Emmaus community, along with questions about our new lifestyle. They also affirmed the arrangement we had with our family.

Most visitors were from World Gospel Church (WGC). Mike and Pat D., who had moved to Indianapolis, came, and Bill connected better than with most visitors. Mike and Bill talked about memories of when we were all at WGC. John and Connie K., both retired, also visited, bought Bill's published books, and rehearsed memories. It was always wonderful to stay in touch with friends.

Our German friend, Stefanie G., a college professor in New Zealand, came a few times in conjunction with conferences. One evening Bill talked about coffee but we thought he meant ice-cream—that we had "a bit of it at breakfast." Finally connecting, we all enjoyed a good laugh. Stefanie exhibited a beautiful connection with Bill—walking around the block together, playing ping-pong, and even arm wrestling, a usual contest when visiting, and Bill always won. Through what she called "table talks," we bonded and lifted up each other in our faith. Stefanie recognized Bill needed more visual interaction.

What's Missing

What have been my sweet sorrows? Bill's loss of memory, loss of ministry, and loss of biblical knowledge stored up. Also I missed the brightness in his hazel eyes. Usually his face had a blank expression, an emptiness. However, the bright light in his eyes did return when he teased me or someone else.

My attitude about the loss of Bill's memory remained raw. But the greatest loss had to be the connection with members of our family: Bill no longer knew how they related to him. Giving up my position meant I was no longer Pastor Bill's wife, even though I still identified as his wife. With this loss of identity, I also experienced a personal loss of connectedness. Instead, I slowly learned to submit to God's will. This continued to be a process, not once and done. My trust in God related to the past, present, and into our future. There's a reason this time is called the present. It is God's gift for us.

Questions for Reflection:

1. What activities does your loved one enjoy? How do you participate?
2. What lessons are difficult for you to learn? How do those change your schedule?
3. What changed about your holidays and visits with family and friends?

Fighting Feelings
and Frustrations

1-10-21—Too often I remained in a performance/ prove myself mode, trying to please others with my actions, then being upset about mistakes. This wintry Sunday I accepted a ride with Becky to church because of snow and ice on the roads. Fine with Bill on the way to church but not afterward; he wanted to leave instead of waiting for family to return home. Bill kept asking why our car was not at church. Outside I lost my patience and shouted, "Okay, I made a mistake!" Our grandson Michael gave us a ride home.

Later Becky encouraged me: "It's hard. It's why we care about this together." I admitted my fear of the unknown, knowing Bill's condition would continue downhill and fretting didn't work when handling all the changes. We were in God's hands. Thus, I needed to be patient and strong in order to endure. God flooded me with peace when my mind stayed on Him. (See Isaiah 26:3.) Oh, to heed God's promises when needed.

Struggling through prayers of confession we recited at church, I placed tension between fact and supposition. Yes, although not perfect in performance and putting myself first, the assurance of salvation was mine. Confessing my sin and pleading forgiveness, reluctantly I sang, "my sins are many." Was that self-righteousness related to my unwillingness to admit faults and failings? Or did I recognize the tension between Wesleyan and Reformed theology, wanting to hold on to tradition versus the truth of my personal experience?

Bill's perfectionist nature often kicked in with cleaning and organizing. A pot or baking dish got extra scrubbing when Bill cleaned, trying to make it sparkle. Often he looked through his desk drawers and re-arranged what's stored there, even if he didn't use things anymore.

One day noticing lights in the garage were on, I turned them off. Again the garage lights were on and I announced to the family I'd turned them off. The next day Becky figured it out. Her dad turned several switches down, not noticing what they controlled. When turning off a light, the switch may be in an up position. Bill passed by later and pushed the switch down. As a solution, Becky turned the switch up in the mud room, leaving the switch in our hallway down. This satisfied Bill's passion to have all switches pointing the "correct" way.

Another day I posted a small note on the back door: "Do not let the dog out before noon." A worker had sprayed trees with chemicals that might harm pets. Bill let our dog out around 10:30 AM, forgetting the posted note and my verbal instructions. This showed he could not be depended on to recall or read something out of the usual routine. Again it's the disease.

2-5-21—One night I had a frightening episode with Bill. He awoke around 2 AM and asked if I would go with him. "No." He then went to the bathroom. Next the closet door opened and Bill stood in the doorway, naked. I told him to put his nightshirt back on. He said he needed to be ready: "They are coming for me." Our exchange went from my telling him to return to bed and his saying he would not.

I handed his nightshirt to him, but he wouldn't cooperate, repeating what he'd been saying. Placing my hands on either side of his face, I said, "You are having a dream and you need to get in bed to finish your dream." He said, "No," refusing to put on his nightshirt. Tears started as I said, "I don't know what to do, how to help you." By then I needed the bathroom. I sat on the toilet and prayed.

Returning to the bedroom, I saw Bill making up his side of the bed. I said, "I'm getting in bed and you ought to go to bed too." I called his attention to the clock; it was now 2:30. I explained one more time he could expect no one to come for him in the middle of the night. Perhaps angels?

I needed help, but wouldn't call Becky or Paul while Bill remained naked. Standing on his side of the bed, I picked up his nightshirt and said, "Bill, put this on for me. Get back in bed and go to sleep." This time he allowed me to help put on his nightshirt. He pulled back the covers and got in bed. Returning to my side of the bed, I placed my hand on his shoulder, and he said, "I'm alright." He stayed on his back several minutes and turned to his right, his usual position for sleeping. Comfortable enough to sleep, I thanked God.

About two hours later, Bill called out, "Mom. Mom." I touched his shoulder and said, "Everything is fine." In the morning nothing was said about the night's episode. Bill probably forgot. I related to Becky what happened, but also asked her advice in case it happened again.

4-10-21—Driving home after a Lenten service, I shouted at Bill, repeating three times something I'd said and he hadn't heard because of not wearing his hearing aids. Often the combination of dementia and hearing loss prompted my getting irritable and frustrated, daily or several times a day. Neither loss of hearing nor memory were his fault, so why get upset? After struggling with confession at church, I had again put myself first before my husband, being irritable instead of loving. I prayed, "Lord, please forgive me . . . again."

At times Bill got stuck on one subject. With Bill in earshot, a friend and I talked about dishwashing, formerly Bill's self-appointed job. Bill added that some men do not think it's their job to do chores around the house. But his mother taught all three sons to clean house, so it became a part of the routine to help me. My friend and I moved on to another subject, but Bill repeated with emphasis that men needed to take on tasks for their family.

7-1-21—Going to Beltone, to have Bill's hearing aids cleaned, turned out to be more than expected. The tech looked in Bill's ears and said they were packed with wax. Out of the left ear he got some dark wax about the size of a small pea. He could not see the eardrum, and that concerned me. The tech said to use peroxide with water to clean out Bill's ears and rinse with warm water each day for a week.

When we arrived home, Bill laid on the couch and I applied the peroxide treatment. He didn't like it but cooperated. After the peroxide bubbled in his ear a few minutes, I used a bulb syringe to extract the solution. The next morning Bill said he could not hear me even when I shouted. Nor could he hear his own voice.

I called our doctor. Mid-afternoon the RN instructed me to continue the procedure with pure peroxide. I asked Bill to get on the couch so we could clean out his ears. He refused, saying he wanted to go to the doctor and have him help. I explained the doctor told me what to do. He said he's going to bed and die, that it didn't matter. I left the room to cry. With Bill sitting in the recliner, it was not a good position to try the treatment.

After dinner, I again asked Bill to get on the couch. He laid on his side for the peroxide treatment. No arguing, no resistance, only a bit befuddled about what I wanted him to do. Since he couldn't hear me or himself or the TV, I shouted that I did it for his own good. In the process, a little wax came out.

Before bedtime, he leaned over the bathroom sink as I poured warm water into the ear canals and let it drain out. Not understanding at first, he allowed the process. The next morning Bill cooperated, so we were off to a good day.

Encouraging Times

In the car on the way to the post office, I inserted a cassette tape to listen to a sermon from Bill, my favorite pastor. As the message began I asked Bill if he recognized the preacher. He said, "He sounds familiar. I know him, can't think of his name." I said he knew that preacher very well. Bill looked puzzled, so I said, "That's you." He uttered something like, "He sounded familiar," and quietly listened to the sermon. Occasionally I'd say, "Good preaching." He agreed with a nod.

Bill liked to go with me when I had several errands to run. While at my hairdresser, he patiently sat while the beautician cut my hair. As I shopped for a casual blouse at Walmart, he followed me around the numerous display racks. No complaints. Driving an unfamiliar route he helped me look for street names, and he checked if cars were nearby as we left a parking space or waited at a stop sign. I also looked; his eyesight wasn't the best.

We ate lunch at Chicago's Pizza, a favorite spot, and Bill especially liked the dessert pizza on the buffet. Stopping at the bank, he stayed in the car as usual. The teller asked me how long we'd been married. When I said 63 years, she replied I must have found a good man. "Yes." Then she wanted me to repeat it to another teller, a newlywed, who asked to reveal my secret. "It's commitment—to the Lord and to each other." Back in the car, I relayed the conversation to Bill. I hadn't told the girls at the bank Bill had memory loss, and although we've changed, our commitment was renewed each day. I not only love who he was but I still love him as he is now. Our marriage vow holds us "for better or worse."

Shortly after we moved to Indianapolis, we had the piano tuned. Such a pleasure to hear Bill play nicely something from memory. Before long that would be put aside. When I'd ask him to play, he refused. It was disappointing to have another enjoyable activity lost to his memory or to resistance.

As we left church one Sunday, a CD played Steve Green singing, *We Have Seen God's Glory.* I believed it connected Bill with his preaching. Before we parked in the garage, I told him, "That's your song. I think of you as I hear those words. When you preach and pray, I see God's glory, Jesus Christ." Others could also testify to this. Bill closed his eyes; perhaps he did feel encouraged.

Sometimes there was an advantage to Bill's loss of memory. Bill filled out a card to be returned to a sweepstakes agency connected with a service organization. He gave it to me for a stamp on the sealed envelope, and on the outside he had checked the box about enclosing a donation. Since the checkbook was not available to him, I assumed he had probably inserted cash from his wallet. I asked if he put any money inside and he didn't remember. So with the envelope set aside to open the next day, I found a 10-dollar bill and returned it to his wallet. I shredded the envelope and reply card, and Bill did not ask about mailing it. I used his loss of memory to my advantage.

Planning Ahead

Bill looked at his desk calendar and asked about the events written there. When he saw I posted my writers conference at Taylor University about an upcoming Friday and Saturday, he asked about that. He donned a sad, neglected face, teasing me. He then asked where Taylor University was located, how far away, and how would I get there. More explanations, but they weren't the last.

While reading Scripture, I decided on some passages that would be good to include in Bill's memorial service, so I added those verses to the file folder marked "Our Funerals." Isaiah 55:11-12 is a good tribute to Bill's preaching, with an emphasis on the Word of God not returning empty. A tribute to his life was also found in Romans, selected verses from chapter 12.

Early in his ministry, Bill chose 2 Timothy 2:15 as a life goal, so that ought to be read. Because of the content, and also the book in the Bible he was most noted for, some prayers from Ephesians should be included. A tribute to marriage and family and church could be read from the fifth chapter in Ephesians. Bill's death might come soon, so while reading these passages, I wanted to record them and be ready.

Family Helpers

Morgan, our grandson Michael's wife, stayed at our house one afternoon while I volunteered at Life Center. Becky arranged this before she and Paul visited his mom in Illinois. I left before Morgan arrived, telling Bill that Morgan would come soon to keep him company. He said he did not need anyone to take care of him. Returning home, I asked if he enjoyed his visit with Morgan. He said, "No one was here." From Morgan I found out she went to the study to tell Grandpa she'd arrived. When Emily came home after teaching school, Morgan left. Emily also greeted Grandpa to say she would be upstairs. Paul and Becky arrived before I returned home. So someone was always here. But Bill did not remember who and when anyone came and left. I decided it was time to give up my volunteer work at Life Center.

I tried not to patronize Bill or instruct him as if he were a child learning new tasks, because it would cause conflict. One night while washing dinner dishes, I asked him to soak a baking dish. He raised his voice to say he already took care of it, for I'm not to tell him what to do. I kept quiet, not pressing the issue.

He generally asked when he needed help. One day he asked me twice where the butter knife belonged. Describing where to put it didn't help, so I showed him where we stored the knife, and he thanked me both times. Would he remember the next time? No. Becky often reminded him we're here to help.

Our son Bill Jr. visited a few days while Becky and Paul went on vacation. This was listed on my husband's calendar, but it didn't surprise me when he asked repeatedly if Bill's wife would come. I said, "No, she has school meetings." I showed him the family photo album Becky made and pointed out the photo of Bill Jr. and Rhonda, calling them by name. He asked how our son is able to stay with us without his wife. Our son hadn't visited us for quite some time, but Bill disagreed, "Yes, he has." Not pushing the issue, instead I pointed out more photos of family members. Handing me the album, Bill said, "Here, this is yours." I said it belonged to him. After I showed him where it was kept, he put it away.

Before our son Bill Jr. returned home, I asked for any observations he'd care to share about his dad and me. He concentrated on my responses, that I'm doing my best and only need to understand the limitations of this situation and our relationship. He agreed every day was new. The previous night gave us proof when his dad prepared the coffee pot ahead for morning. He put six cups of water in the pot with two scoops of coffee. I told Bill to add two more scoops so it could be stronger. That didn't compute; if our usual two scoops for four cups were correct, then four scoops would need eight cups of water. Bill added more water. When relating the incident to Becky, she reminded me her dad's logic is skewed, his reasoning skills damaged.

Early one morning I put two letters from the mailbox on Bill's desk. Surprised, shocked, and amused, I saw black streaks all over his face made by a Sharpie marker. We went to wash his face, but Becky first took a photo to send to her brothers. John asked, "What did he say?" Becky texted John that their dad said, "I don't do such. Somebody did this." To which John replied, "Something a toddler would say." Yes, we'd heard that often from our children: "I didn't do that. He/she did it." Bill had only me to blame. At least we all got a good laugh. No use asking Bill how it happened. My guess: he was shaving with the black marker while at his desk.

Bill gave me another fundraising piece of mail addressed to him, with a request to sign up and send a donation. Determined we wouldn't send a gift, I told him it would only mean more mailings sent to us. He pointed out it's a good cause, and while in agreement, I stated we were still not going to contribute. The conversation got heated when he asked that we be dropped from their mailing list. Gladly, but it didn't satisfy him, saying we might as well not donate to anyone. I asked if we should not support the church or missionaries. He said something like, all or none. We donated to those we had decided to support, and we could be selective. He ended by saying I could do what I wanted with my money, so I pressed it no further.

Why did I keep disagreeing with him? While not trying to reason with Bill was best, I still attempted, especially when he started the conversation. They usually turned out poorly, so I put the fundraising letter aside to toss later. He'd forget about it.

Confusion had become a daily occurrence with Bill. One morning after he finished breakfast, Bill handed me a folded-up milk carton, asking if we had more. I showed him two cartons of vanilla-flavored almond milk in the refrigerator. Not satisfied, he asked what he ate for breakfast. I opened the pantry and took out his favorite cereal, Cocoa Puffs. He was convinced we had what he wanted for his next breakfast. Later Bill expressed concern about the family buying what we used. I explained, "I write a check to Becky every month for groceries." Satisfied again. End of discussion and confusion. Until the next time.

"What time are we leaving? Where are we going? How will we get there?" I answered his questions the umpteenth time while Bill's repetitions grated my nerves. His questions and my answers continued. The sound of my response may be sweet-tempered, but it didn't reflect my inner spirit. Why was I frustrated? Why was I viewing his repetitions as irritations? It's because they interrupted *my* thoughts, *my* activities, *my* desires.

I should endeavor to rearrange my desires and be considerate of the husband I love and want to please. My commitment to love did not depend on circumstances. Love lasts through the hard times, and it may hurt. When putting aside my way, I made room in my personal space for Bill, his loss of memory, and his interests. If I focused on him and our love, those repetitions wouldn't erupt in an irritable way, but enable me to be his helpmate. I admit that being submissive to Bill was easier when he had the mental capacity to lead. Now it's more difficult with Bill's memory loss, erratic behavior, and how he got fixated on things such as cleaning crumbs off a table, even at a restaurant.

Because Bill began dozing off more in the daytime, I reported to Becky who asked about his medications. He'd been taking an allergy pill at lunchtime to curb his runny nose. We omitted the medication and noticed he was not taking as many naps. Most evenings while watching TV or a movie, Bill would doze, and I debated whether to nudge him or let him be. Those naps during the day didn't affect his sleeping at night. He got around seven to eight hours and usually up only once for a bathroom break.

At the registration counter for six-month checkups with our PCP, the nurse asked Bill for his date of birth. He looked at me, and I recited the date. Another item forgotten. The lab drew blood from Bill to keep track of his liver enzymes. The doctor questioned Bill about hobbies, but Bill didn't understand, and he'd left his hearing aids at home. I spoke up about his being bored and needed suggestions. The doctor said that Bill should play the piano; it would be "good for mind and hands." Unfortunately, later Bill had no recollection of doctor's orders. We press on.

Questions for Reflection:

1. How do you focus on the positives and encouraging times?
2. Have you made plans for the future and how people will be involved?
3. How are you handling (fighting against) unwanted feelings?

Focus on Faith

A. W. Tozer wrote about a pastor being the same man in the pulpit as when "talking to someone about the common affairs of life" (*The Pursuit of God Bible*). That described my preacher-husband. No whitewash, no deception in or out of the pulpit. Integrity had been his practice in ministry and at home. Committed to biblical truth, Bill always preached and lived his messages with total honesty.

The Lord also gave Ezekiel the authority to speak His word to the people in exile and that he follow it whether or not they listened (Ezekiel, chapters 2 and 3). A. W. Tozer wrote of the "authority in the pulpit," because people recognized that and were responsible. The apostle Paul had God's authority: "we speak as those approved by God to be entrusted with the gospel" (1 Thessalonians 2:4).

Bill had gifts, given by God who called him to preach when 18 years old, and he prepared himself to know and preach the truth. When he taught from the New Testament, he built on Old Testament foundations. Not only had he earned degrees in education and practiced diligence in studies, God anointed his teaching. Like the apostle Paul, Bill's ministry encouraged people, urging them "to live lives worthy of God" (1 Thessalonians 2:12). Church members listened to Bill's exposition of the Bible, and were challenged to obey God. Nothing persuaded the apostle Paul or Bill to back down from God's truth.

"Don't let anyone look down on you because you are young, but set an example for the believers in speech, in conduct, in love, in faith and in purity" (1 Timothy 4:12). Bill began his ministry at age 20, and that's why he liked Paul's letters to Timothy. "Fan into flame the gift of God" (2 Timothy 1:6). "For the Spirit God gave us does not make us timid, but gives us power, love and self-discipline" (v. 7). God gifted Bill, and he had never been timid when preaching the truth of the gospel. Truth demanded a response—to accept or reject.

Bill's faith definitely gave me no concern; it remained part of his identity. Even in his subconscious state, he recited a testimony about his life and what's important. How did I know this? Mainly, he talked in his sleep. It centered on doing what was right. In his dream, he either preached before a crowd or talked to one person: "Do what's right. That's what I do." Praise Jesus! In his prayers—grace at meals and at bedtime—he repeated, "Thank You, Lord, for all Your gifts: our family, our home, our food. All You give us is good. Thank You."

While reading Psalm 112, Bill's generosity came to my mind: "Good will come to those who are generous and lend freely, who conduct their affairs with justice. Surely the righteous will never be shaken . . . . Their hearts are steadfast, trusting in the LORD" (vv. 5, 6, 7). Bill desired justice, always willing to give of himself.

When I got up one morning I thought Bill said something to me, but he was talking in his sleep—to someone. Then he said, "Let's pray" and started a prayer as I left the room. Even in his sleep, his faith was evident.

One evening several men from church met for Bible study in our home. Afterward Paul told me Bill spoke about his health and memory loss, including how grateful he'd been for life's blessings. When I asked Bill about their meeting, he only said, "I just sat there." I was glad he did speak up as Paul reported. During Sunday school he rarely contributed to the discussion, and when he did speak, he returned to a previous topic.

I became passionate about publishing Bill's messages, seeking to provide materials to enhance the ministry of the Church, and encourage the moral acceptance of truth. Just like Ezekiel, Tozer, and Paul, Bill recognized "the strong hand of the Lord" on his life (see Ezekiel 3:14). Preparing Bill's sermons for publication kept me motivated. This determination to publish his sermons followed his diagnosis of dementia.

My friend, Beth S., led a Bible study at her church on Psalm 103, "Do not Forget: Remember the Goodness of God." Her introduction to the study included Bill and his forgetfulness. I quote Beth:

"When I think about forgetting, it reminds me of Ann, a precious friend whose husband suffered from Alzheimer's disease. So much from Bill's past he could not recall. He didn't remember his preaching career that spanned decades. He didn't remember being a student of Hebrew linguistics in graduate school and a professor of Greek in a Christian college. He didn't remember many of the people from his past with whom he once had a close relationship.

"Ann took message notes from his sermon series to publish in book format. She listened to the audio recordings of his preaching to edit his transcripts for the book.

"For several days Ann listened to the recording, and her husband Bill said, 'Who is that talking?'

"My friend replied every time, 'I am listening to my favorite preacher.'

"He always looked surprised. 'Oh, who is it?' Genuinely curious.

"She compassionately stated, 'It's you.'

"'Oh,' with flat affect he asked, 'Am I good?'

"Ann always affirmed, 'Oh yes. You were the best.' And they had this conversation every day for weeks. Bill didn't remember the day before. He didn't recognize his own voice. He no longer recalled a single Hebrew or Greek word he had once taught.

"In the early stage Bill knew he didn't remember well. The rock, the spiritual foundation of their family, no longer remembered who he was or what he did.

"And I wonder, aren't we at times guilty of the same thing when it comes to God? Sometimes we don't remember who God is or what He has done for us even though we lived it and experienced it personally. How heartbreaking that must be to God when we forget, when we have short memories of His faithfulness. The Lord said, 'Do not forget.'

"My friend's husband didn't have a choice. Dementia stole his memory. But we can choose to remember. We should not forget the goodness of God, even in the silent seasons of life, even in the waiting, even in the storm. Maybe especially in those times: 'Do not forget.'"

Thank you, Beth.

What seemed like my impossible dream became a reality, including four published books and a continuing podcast of Bill's sermons from his last church (WGC). These provide a legacy and proclaimed God's Word. All total he preached for 55 years, and I worked on completing the task God had given Bill. God had been in this from the beginning.

Bill may have believed he no longer had an influence in personal relationships. Yet friends wrote about his positive impact on their lives. At church and in stores Bill readily spoke to strangers (adults and children): "Hello, how are you?" People related back to him as he smiled. The main path of contributing influence became delegated to his published books and online podcast. It's why I continued to pursue these avenues—to keep his influence going. Wisdom remained current in those messages he delivered before retirement.

During his dementia, Bill's prayers were about pleasing God. Bill delivered what Becky and I called "talks." Although we did not understand most of what he said, we could count on two repeated topics: doing what's right and doing what's good. Those phrases were heard when he talked either to me or other members of the family. I also heard this repeated while Bill slept, as if he were preaching. Reading Scripture, I found these same mandates in both the Old and New Testaments. In Bill's podcasts, he repeated those phrases. I can only conclude without a doubt: Bill's faith had always been based on what's right and what's good.

Doing what's right was also reflected in my commitments. As noted earlier, I had volunteered at Southside Life Center. They scheduled an in-service with breakfast at a volunteer's home. I wavered about going; no one would be home with Bill. Paul would be driving Becky to Chicago, on her way to Brazil, South America, to visit Chrissa, their daughter, her husband, and his family. None of the grandkids were available. Becky expressed hesitance about my leaving her dad by himself; even a phone call might confuse him. Since moving to Indianapolis, we had not left Bill alone. After thinking I'd risk it, I decided to stay home. Better choice—be here with Bill and take myself off the throne.

More Changes

Lately we noticed a lack of senses such as taste. Bill ate certain foods he once did not like. He even ate liver. Also absent was his sense of smell: no fragrance to a rose. Some of these changes meant adjustments. Becky always proved helpful about what to expect.

7-17-22—Bill's body temperature remained cool, even in the summer heat; and since his desk chair was near the vent, the air conditioning blew directly onto him. Adding a space heater under

Bill's desk helped. Twice, however, I found it turned on when he was away from the desk. One night I checked on the heater. Sure enough, it was on.

When we watched TV in the evenings, he would always spread a blanket over us. Fine with me, especially while eating ice cream. He also liked to rub my leg; and Becky teased us, saying, "It's no secret what you do under the blanket while sitting together."

9-28-22—One Monday morning I noticed a cut and a bruise on Bill's face. Of course, he couldn't explain how he got those. I set out to put together what happened. Several items I found misplaced in the living room: one moved from the bookshelf to the piano; another on the coffee table from the piano. Nothing broken. On one of his trips from the bathroom during the night, he probably got confused and turned left instead of right, ending up in the living room. He probably stumbled and fell in the dark, hitting his head on the piano or coffee table. Surprisingly, I had slept through it all. Later Becky agreed with my assumptions.

Bill went with me for my scheduled haircut, and he sat in a corner chair. I put my purse on the floor nearby. When I turned toward him, he was holding tightly to my purse as if to protect it. This also happened as he sat across from me in our podiatrist's exam room. He was still my protector.

10-1-22—This morning Bill didn't want to swallow his Co-Q-10 capsule. What he said made no sense, and he kept pouring water on it while saying "No," and I got upset. He asked me what to do, and in a grumpy tone I said, "Throw it in the trashcan."

That evening Bill put up quite a fuss about taking a shower. Is it worth the struggle? I made the mistake of saying he only bathed once a week. He insisted differently, shaking his finger at me. His mind was probably in the past, so we disagreed. With an angry tone he told me to leave as he got in the tub. Afterward he looked cheerful, and when I asked if he was clean, he smiled. In the morning he awoke with a loud, "No, No!" What had he dreamed?

The following Saturday Bill was more agreeable about taking a shower, but cleaning his denture proved a problem. Bill smeared shaving cream over it and repeated, "I've done it this way all the time." I tried to reason with him. Finally giving in, I let him keep the shaving cream on his denture and changed it later. Becky had repeatedly told me to stop trying to reason with her dad. He was no longer capable of reasoning. Thus, it was hard for me to let go.

10-10-22—Becky showed me how her dad placed the narrow juice glasses in the silverware drawer among the knives. Another new habit developed during dinner: Bill separated food so none touched each other on his plate, which we found amusing to watch.

Playing solitaire with him could be gratifying and yet puzzling; he forgot the rules for Klondike and wanted to play his own way, moving the Aces down and putting black cards on black. He said, "It all changed today." When playing with him, he gave me hints about what to move. He showed no objection to my playing his games, and it actually pleased us both to play solitaire together.

11-21-22—It's 6:50 on Sunday morning and I awoke to find Bill fully dressed with coat and hat on, sleeping in his chair in front of his computer. He had turned the overhead light and fan on. I took a photo. I slept through it all, not knowing he had gotten up and dressed in church clothes. Last night, refusing to take a shower, he said he'd do it in the morning. Not now! When I sent the photo to Becky, she replied, "He outsmarted you!" Yes, whether it was intentional, who's to say?

Anger Issues

11-22-22—Bill got mad at Becky. He refused to move away from the kitchen sink which had a plumbing problem. Bill shouted at Becky, "Leave!" She softly said, "No, you leave." Repeated explanations to leave the sink alone weren't effective—until I persuaded Bill to turn around and go with me to the laundry room where he could dry dishes as I washed them in the laundry sink.

11-25-22—Becky prepared a wonderful Thanksgiving meal. Present were ten adults, three children, and three dogs. Bill didn't interact much during their visit. As we sat at the table, Bill dozed off once, and I nudged him to wake up. Our son said, "Let sleeping dogs lie." That was not funny to me, but disrespectful.

11-28-22—Lately Bill has been more insistent on having his way. Yesterday he put a small pinecone onto his dinner plate. He took it from the autumn centerpiece on the table. Becky told her dad he would not like eating a pinecone. He reacted by pointing his finger at her, saying he knew what he wanted. She said, "Go ahead and eat the pinecone." We laughed as I removed the pinecone. Becky took the basket off the table. It was not always easy to be patient with him.

One night Bill pointed his finger at me, saying, "I know what I always do." The issue involved wearing his underwear under his nightshirt to bed. I finally persuaded him to take off his underwear, because I wanted him to wear a fresh Depends. It was difficult not to "correct" him. If we were telling him what to do, he would get angry. The way we phrased our requests or persuaded him needed to be tempered with kindness.

Bill would talk on and on about any given subject. I paused a film on TV and entered the kitchen to dish ice cream as our snack. Bill followed me, talking the whole while. The best I could understand, he spoke about something "bad and we needed to correct it." Perhaps it was about the ugly creatures in the animated film.

11-29-22—Bill didn't want to keep our appointment to have our toenails clipped by the podiatrist. He said we could do it ourselves, but that hasn't worked well. His toenails bled when I trimmed them. Becky suggested giving her dad a Benadryl before we left, perhaps to relax him. We agreed to keep our appointment. The doctor said acting as if it hurts is common with patients who have dementia.

12-4-22—Returning to church after Covid, we had communion served by deacons up front. It did not go well with Bill. He took the bread and then poured the juice into his hand, spilling the juice onto the floor. It embarrassed me, yet the servers showed compassion. During the preaching Bill dozed off and made motions with his hands when he woke up. Did we need to sit in the back? But Becky said I'm the only one who's concerned about disturbing people. New friends came to our pew with hugs and greetings. As I introduced them to Paul after the service, the wife stated she liked to see us in our same seats every Sunday morning.

Her words helped me feel the issue was settled. We continued to sit in our usual place—three rows from the front on the right.

1-29-23—Bill had some occasions of Sundowner's Syndrome. This condition, often related to dementia, usually caused confusion, getting nighttime and daytime mixed up, including agitation as night approached. It affects one's ability to reason and focus on reality. Bill became unusually demanding.

Some evenings he either acted as if 6 PM was time for bed (although we had not had dinner yet), or he was not ready to go to bed at 10 o'clock. The confusion usually occurred when we didn't follow routine. That evening instead of watching TV together, Bill played solitaire on his computer, not his usual evening routine. When it was time for bed, he at first did not want to undress. Thus getting ready for bed turned into a long frustrating process. Our routine was important that both of us follow it.

2-4-23—Becky moved the canister of peppermints onto a lower level in the closet. She had read that those with dementia often don't look down. That's also why we positioned the security locks down low on our two hallway doors. The theory didn't work, however, as we walked in parking lots where Bill would look down and pick up trash.

One afternoon Bill and I walked from the car to the theater to view an episode of *The Chosen,* season three. During most of the film Bill kept his eyes closed and also dozed, true to Becky's prediction when I'd told her my plan. Choosing not to disturb Bill, I enjoyed the film. But I kept a disgruntled attitude as we headed home. Thankfully, further into the evening my attitude improved.

2-5-23—I personally related to the prayer at church about "harsh words." At night I uttered harsh words at Bill, wanting him to understand and agree to bedtime. Our kids said I expected too much and didn't face what's real. Deep down I wanted Bill to give me some measure of hope, to know he was present, underneath all the dementia and confusion. Learning came slowly as I would disconnect expectations from reality.

Yesterday and today were spoiled by a bad attitude, harsh words, disappointment, not facing reality, being angry at myself and those I love. These were all lingering remnants of my bad attitude. I cried out to God, confessed again and received His forgiveness again. I'm thankful God is always patient with me.

Adjusting to Changes

Because Bill's Bible study habits changed over the years, I adapted new routines to hear God's Word and to pray together. When we first moved to Indianapolis, our former church sent Bill a devotional guide in the mail and he read it every morning. With a reminder, he looked up the Scripture. That routine lasted only a little over a year. Occasionally he got out his Bible and looked at it, but he had lost recognition of most words.

In bed at night we'd hold hands and take turns offering a prayer. Before saying "goodnight," I asked Bill if he wanted to pray. Often he didn't understand. I repeated the invitation, but he remained quiet. So I said, "Amen," and kissed him. From then on, I said the bedtime prayer without asking him.

During breakfast I used a Bible app with a daily Scripture read by a pastor or known Christian personality. The app included a lesson and a prayer to recite. This practice satisfied me, but Bill's expression never registered much appreciation. He did listen to the verse and closed his eyes in prayer.

Because of Becky's encouragement and her suggestions for needed technical tasks, Bill's podcast started and ran efficiently. Every Wednesday during a meal, Bill and I listened to each new episode on my phone. These episodes reflected how Bill preached biblical truth, put in the research, and unashamedly added his comments and personal illustrations. As we listened, I was again filled with respect and admiration for my husband the preacher. Bill liked to see his photo icon on my phone, and he smiled when he recognized himself and heard his preaching.

3-12-23—Changes happened with Bill's leisure time, such as when he forgot other computer games and only understood Spider solitaire. As he tried Klondike, the red and black cards confused him. Also Bill was dozing more frequently. As he sat beside me to watch a Western on TV, he closed his eyes, snored, and muttered noises. When I asked if he were watching, he would say, "I'm listening." He did rouse when the music woke him.

3-13-23—Before Sunday lunch I asked Becky if I could help. She said, "Yes, you can help with baby-sitting," referring to her dad. After lunch Bill again got in the way of the dishwashing chore. He used the washcloth to dry the dishes. So Becky needed to re-wash them. We hid the dishtowel, because Bill occasionally wiped his nose on it. I asked Bill to follow me into our study to be out of the way while Becky cleaned up the kitchen. I wanted to help like we used to do, but Bill's lack of cleanliness made it unwise to continue that practice.

Occasionally when family members and friends gathered in the family room, I would choose to stay in our living room. This sometimes made me feel like an outsider, but Bill was unaware. I wasn't bit-ter; Bill came first. I realized that in the future he'd be gone and I would miss those days, assuming he would die before me.

3-21-23—My friend, John W., invited me to be a guest on his podcast. As an attempt to be ready early, I had laid out Bill's dress pants and he put them on. After breakfast, Bill came out of the bathroom, holding his pants open. He said, "water," because he had wet his pants. This created added time to change his clothes. I lost my temper along with my patience. I chose his black jeans, but it was difficult to tighten the waistband due to his weight gain. I said he was getting fat, but he gave no reaction. Perhaps he didn't hear me. I unreasonably blamed Bill for my ill temper.

Getting dressed, I changed my mind about what I'd wear, thinking, it's only a podcast, who will see me? Later I found out it would also be on YouTube. Anxiety increased about my appearance, but Bill's published books had prompted the podcast invite.

A friend from church, Glenn M., volunteered to drive Bill and me to Mooresville where the Focus on Christ podcast would be recorded. As we traveled, changes in the route due to construction on the interstate sparked my gratitude for Glenn's gift of transport. We enjoyed brief conversation along the way, and Bill liked the ride, constantly looking out the windows from the back seat.

Inside the church's recording room, we met the two podcast hosts, Jack E. and John W., and a third person who operated the microphones and cameras. Bill and Glenn sat near the cameraman. I took a seat at the table with my script, but I'd not need it, mainly because the hosts didn't ask *my* questions. They especially wanted details about our conversion experiences and marriage.

Jack and John also asked about my caregiving experience, and I related events, problems, and special moments. This exchange was aimed at caregivers who might be listening to their podcast. On the air they thanked Becky and Paul for how they also committed themselves to caregiving. As planned, we talked about Bill's books and the publishing process connected to our faith journey. We highlighted each book, especially *Words of Endearment* and *Scandal of Christmas*. I plugged Bill's books and podcast and how people might contact me. Answering the hosts' off-the-cuff questions, I was satisfied with my first guest appearance on a podcast, which aired after Easter.

4-9-23—Becky and Paul were visiting his mother in Illinois. Bill cooperated with my decision to go to the early worship service on Easter Sunday to hear the choir. Before we left we only had coffee, but I planned a bigger than usual breakfast after we returned home. First I chose to sit in the center section, but it didn't suit Bill. He pointed over to our usual seats, so we moved. At the early service they did not dim the lights over the congregation, and that helped Bill stay alert. Worship service was grand as we sang familiar Easter hymns.

Returning home, we had breakfast of eggs, sausage, and toast. Around 2:30 I started dinner: sweet potatoes in the oven, ham steak, and broccoli. Later Bill wanted to "go somewhere." Too often I put him off, but today being Easter, we drove out in the country and even brought along the dog for the fun of it. One day—sooner or later—we wouldn't be able to take such trips.

4-11-23—When it got harder for Bill to be ready to go anywhere, I gave him more time and checked on how he dressed himself. An example: he put his underwear on while still wearing nighttime Depends. Planning ahead helped, carving out enough time to get both of us ready. Some of the time (not always) when I watched Bill dress or undress, he resisted any change made in the routine. His usual remark, "I always do this," led me to give yet another unwelcome correction.

If Bill got to the kitchen before me, I assumed whatever he did could be undone later. That was too optimistic. One such time Bill showed me a cereal bowl with about a dozen purple grapes hidden in coffee grounds. I found it to be quite funny.

His perceived use of this concoction escaped me. After taking a photo to send to our kids, I removed the grapes from the coffee so I could use both.

Night time brought surprises almost regularly, and 4 AM seemed to be the set alarm in Bill's mind. One night I noticed Bill was not in bed, then I saw him getting dressed in the walk-in closet. Avoiding the word "morning," I said instead, "It's four o-clock in the middle of the night and you need to come back to bed." Bill had dressed in three layers, putting on a long-sleeved dress shirt over a short-sleeved polo-shirt over his T-shirt. I tried persuading him to change into his usual nightshirt, but his verbal and physical reactions were nonsensical. Eventually he returned to bed as I put away the clothes he had gotten out. We were able to sleep three more hours.

5-12-23—Bill ate hot cereal this morning and my reaction wasn't good. I had left the kitchen to put out-going letters in the mailbox, and when I returned Bill was pouring coffee onto his Cocoa Puffs. I hollered, "Stop! Don't! No!" All poor choices of words toward someone with dementia. These negative words produced the reaction I expected: "What? Why?" Refusing to give me the coffee pot, he took it to the counter. I told him, "Eat your cereal while it's hot," rubbing in his mistake.

5-16-23—Saturday night became my appointed time for Bill's shower. With a fresh haircut, he would be more easily persuaded to bathe. I'd explain, "Before I can cut your hair, you need to take off most of your clothes," but this time it was not computing. We used motions, and finally he took off his shirt. It was like talking to a toddler with limited vocabulary. The haircut went well, and Bill gave no argument about bathing.

"Those People"

During one of Bill's talkative days, most of the afternoon and into dinner time, he kept mentioning "those people," and "not doing that anymore." I had no idea as to the context. When I asked if he referred to preaching, he shook his head and said, "No." Later Bill talked with Paul about the same subject. Though not understanding, Paul smiled and nodded.

As we sat down for dinner, Bill stuck his fork onto the serving platter to pick-up a piece of fish to move to his plate. I corrected him, explaining we were to wait for the blessing. In the process of stopping his action, I spilled half of his iced tea onto his empty plate, his jeans, and the floor. While Becky and Paul cleaned up my mess, Bill was more concerned about his wet jeans. We spread a towel over his lap which seemed to satisfy. After dinner, Bill headed to the bedroom to change from his wet clothes, including a fresh long-sleeved jersey shirt, but he had not put on dry underwear.

Getting ready for bed, Bill didn't take off his T-shirt. After several attempts to explain, with Bill saying it's what he always does, I handed him the nightshirt. So in the morning, he was wearing the same T-shirt. I too often tried to explain to Bill what he "should" do, but that only evoked irritation. It's a lesson I needed repeatedly. I wanted to do things as we had done them. I know routine is good, but my persistence often led to conflict.

5-19-23—During Bill's visit to his neurologist, the doctor generally asked if Bill still dressed himself. I explained this process was fluid, meaning the changes did not come quickly, consistently, or drastically. I added details: "Before getting in bed, I would lay out clothes for Bill to wear the following day. We dressed in our walk-in closet where a cedar chest was stored and useful as a seat. For weekdays, his clothes consisted of underwear with pads, a jersey shirt and jeans. Socks and belts were kept on nearby shelves and his shoes on the floor. Periodically I checked on Bill to ask if he needed help."

One morning he put on his shirt before his T-shirt, and I asked him to change. He surprised me another day by taking the pad out of his underpants, so I added one later in the day. It was only cautionary at this stage, because he did not need one every day. Even though I had his jeans ready, he may choose dress pants. I objected partly because they would probably be soiled later with food. But most likely it was how I wanted it.

I soon dreaded Saturday nights, due to my desire that Bill shower at least once a week. His objection made no sense to me, but Becky suggested her dad probably had no knowledge what to do once in the bathtub. There were too many steps involved in the process of bathing. When I offered help, he said, "no," voiced often as I urged him to bathe. Other words he uttered I didn't understand. Encouraging him to be clean, I reminded him tomorrow was Sunday and we'd attend church. This whole procedure became a battle of the wills, and most often he won.

Meal time, especially supper, could be a scene of disgruntled behavior, and not always from Bill. Before a meal was ready, he called my attention and pointed to his mouth. He wanted to eat and now. For my satisfaction, I told Bill that Becky was in charge of supper. I then turned back to work on a writing assignment.

If we had leftovers, I could prepare a meal to serve ourselves. He observed the selections I placed on the counter, and I asked him to choose. Our sons said it wasn't necessary to ask. To me, it seemed proper. Placing servings on our plates worked well to eat early and please Bill. He asked, however, where were "those people." We both preferred we eat as a family.

When either Becky or I prepared a meal, Bill liked to watch. We also needed to watch him. He often reached for an item, and we couldn't count on his hands being clean. We used the kitchen island to prepare food—either sandwiches for lunch, or more involved if supper. Bill stood by and watched every move.

At breakfast, Bill ate the same cereal, Cocoa Puffs. After he poured cereal into his bowl, I'd bring the milk to the table and pour it there. I didn't trust him to carry the bowl with milk. If I wasn't watching, Bill may pour juice or iced tea on his cereal. He would not complain if I didn't empty the bowl to start over. It was Cocoa Puffs with whatever liquid.

Recognition

5-20-23—Supper was later than usual, so Becky sent Bill to call me to eat. He actually spoke correctly. I headed to the dinner table. What happened next proved Bill's confusion and lack of recognition. As Becky brought food to the table, Bill reluctantly sat down, looked at me, then left to fetch me. Insisting I had already arrived did not register with Bill. He headed back to our study. Becky said he went to get me, but I wasn't sure what he was doing. When he returned, he was surprised to see me sitting there. Teasing, I said, "I beat you here." Talking with Becky later, she related a few days earlier when she called out "Dad" as he headed to the back door. She wanted him to know the dog was with her in the family room. Bill either didn't recognize his name or did not hear her call.

Recognition resumed later, and I told Becky her dad allowed me to come to bed with him. Some mornings when I would wake Bill, I'd stand by his side of the bed, tap him on the shoulder, and call out his name. With eyes wide open, he looked at me standing by the bed, then divert his attention to my side of the bed. Perhaps he wanted to make sure it was his wife talking to him.

Curious, I doubted he would recognize our sons John and Tom who planned to stay with us in June while Becky and Paul worked at church camp. Also our granddaughter, Anna, her husband, Michael, and their triplets scheduled a visit the following weekend. Would Bill recognize these family members?

5-21-23—This Sunday morning I had to search for Bill's clothes I had placed on top of the cedar chest. I woke Bill and asked where he put his clothes. Of course, no reply. He had not dressed yet.

After another quick search in our bedroom, I went to our study.

On Bill's computer chair there were his clothes, wadded up, not neat. On top of his desk were hats and a pair of gloves from the coat closet, framed photos from a desk nearby, and a small photo album. He'd scattered potpourri from a red glass container onto the other desk. In the living room was a cup holder with his pens and a small wooden cross, usually on Bill's desk. Regrettably, I didn't take a photo, but put everything back in place, along with the clothes Bill would wear to church. During the early morning hours, Bill had moved items as I again slept through it all.

5-24-23—One evening I prepared chef salads for our supper. Bill stood by the center island to watch the process. Later, before bedtime, I found Bill's hearing aids on his desk to move to the charger. But I also saw three colorful mini bell peppers graced his desk, probably seized from the kitchen counter as I prepared our salads. He must have liked the colors or wanted to have a snack later. I showed them to Paul and he asked, "What?" I said, "I found these on Dad's desk," and Paul shook his head.

I had started putting our mail in the mailbox, but instead one morning I asked Bill to go to the mailbox with an anniversary card I wanted to mail. He pointed outside and I confirmed the direction.

A few minutes later Becky found my card on a kitchen counter when she noticed her dad forcefully trying to close the open screen door off the sunporch. My mistake. I had left it ajar so Jules, our dog, could come in while I went to the bathroom. The door could have broken, but thankfully Becky heard it. Why would Bill choose the route through the back sunporch to go to the mailbox out front? Another mystery. After bringing my card to the mailbox, I returned to the house and Bill clapped for me. He's my happy camper.

Expectations

Convicted again of my sour attitude toward Bill, I understood the reason behind it. Expectations! I expected Bill to be like he once was, the man I've admired. This mindset affected my attitude and tone of voice. I was both sad for Bill and angry with how I reacted. Our children often said I had unreasonable expectations about their dad, and they were correct. I desperately needed to diminish my expectations and cast out fear of the future.

Expectations must decrease in my mind in order to show in my actions. Roman Emperor Marcus Aurelius is noted to have said, "You have power over your mind—not outside events. Realize this, and you will find strength." I continued to work on releasing those thoughts which caused irritation in me and toward others.

5-30-23—Bill insisted on folding every cloth in his reach, including the hand towel and washcloths in the bathroom and the dishtowels in the kitchen. I resolved not to re-fold them, unless Bill had folded the hand towel tightly into a small square and I couldn't dry my hands. His method of folding varied—sometimes in thirds, fourths, or a square. I quit refolding these linens simply because they were not the way I wanted.

Did it matter? No. So I became more comfortable with Bill's folding process. It became a mind-changer as well as freeing me from re-doing his actions. Included was how he straightened items around the house, whether the wooden cross or book on the coffee table or chairs in the foyer. I admit I sometimes moved an object, only to watch Bill change it back, setting straight what had been put at an angle.

Vocabulary continued to cause difficulties, not only with Bill's understanding what I said, but he had forgotten more spoken words. I'd point to his bedtime pill on the night stand and say, "Take your pill." Instead, he pointed to a decorative pillow on the floor. Pillow for pill. Such an understandable mistake. More words were lost from his memory bank. One evening I asked him to grab the

Afghan blanket, a usual request as we sat on the dual recliner and watched TV in our living room. Instead of the blanket, he placed a blue pillow on his lap. By his expression, I'd not made a simple request, so I returned the pillow and grabbed the blanket. He looked pleased.

6-6-23—Another morning while preparing breakfast, I came in and out of the kitchen. I discovered several mysterious incidents. First, Bill had opened a bag of chips and placed some on his cloth napkin. I put those back. Next he had served up his Cocoa Puffs, but placed three spoons next to his bowl.

As usual I had put our little plastic cups on the table which held morning meds, but Bill's cup was empty. As I poured milk over his cereal and he started eating, I discovered the pills in his bowl. By then it was too late to correct; some pills had dissolved and he had sucked the medicine from one capsule. What would one day without prescriptions matter? I found coffee spilled onto the floor and a saucer filled with coffee in front of the coffee pot. Of course, Bill denied knowing how any of that happened. His words, "I did not." Wiping up the coffee, I lost my temper.

Reflecting later, was I expecting family members to hear and sympathize with how I spoke to Bill? This was another problem to work on. I would be uncomfortable if others in the house heard how I reacted in frustration. When expressing myself in a raised voice, usually Bill cared little about what I'd said. Again this highlighted how I was being self-focused.

6-8-23—When I faced the reality of Bill's level of understanding, it proved to be similar to making adjustments suitable for a child. I acted like his parent, and often confronted the main difference between a toddler and a person with dementia—that he was no longer teachable. I liked the way Allie Sgro, a licensed nursing assistant (LNA), wrote: "Unlike toddlers, who are constantly learning something new, people with dementia are constantly *losing* something—an ability, a word, a memory, a bit of themselves" (*Guideposts*, Aug/Sept 2022).

One morning I visually recognized this difference as I informed Bill our son John had installed the Mine Sweep game on his computer. Not interested in starting the game, Bill tried to communicate by moving one hand over his head and saying, "Past." His knowledge of the game stayed in the past, and he couldn't bring it back. I pulled up his Spider solitaire and an unfinished game appeared. With a big smile, Bill sat in front of the computer to finish the game he had started.

John and Tom were here four days while Becky and Paul worked out of town at youth camp. As my usual practice at the end of their visits, I asked each one their observations and any advice. John indicated that his dad's dementia had moved "up a notch." He also gave a suggestion for a better word choice: use "bring" instead of "take." John had not followed through on my earlier request—to play ping pong with his dad. John said playing ping pong was a useless endeavor. John advised me to allow his dad to do whatever pleased him, such as watching cartoons. It needed no plot or objective, only enjoyment, and this related also to the games on his computer. If he's satisfied with the one Spider solitaire, it wasn't necessary to introduce other games simply for variety.

Tom suggested I buy items suitable for people with dementia, such as a special blanket with sensory objects. That would match with how Bill helped with laundry each week, but I didn't follow through on Tom's idea.

While John and Tom visited, Bill did not interact directly. Once Bill moved closely to face John, said something, and then giggled. Another time Bill gave us a long talk about what's right. Trying to direct Bill to interact didn't work, like when our sons were ready to leave, Bill stayed in his office chair. He did not go to them for hugs; they had to come to him. And he didn't follow me to their car to wave goodbye. I tried not to let it bother me; it had become his way.

Tone of Voice

6-9-23—I slowly made a transition of adjusting my tone of voice. The old myth stated: if you speak louder, the person will hear, understand, and follow instructions. That doesn't work well for the elderly, nor was it effective for someone with dementia. Speaking louder elicited no improvement in Bill's understanding, no matter how much I hoped it would.

Friday was my designated laundry day. After I placed dirty clothes in baskets to bring to the laundry room, Bill would often fold some items on the way to be washed. Later I brought the clean clothes to the bedroom, and together we folded towels and underwear. Bill folded his share, and while they were not the way I'd typically fold them, I didn't refold before placing them in his chest-of-drawers. I smiled at how he folded cloth napkins for the dinner table. He created several unique shapes. Family members could adjust their own napkins if they chose. After we finished folding laundry, Bill helped me put away clean linens in the closet. I recognized his need to be helpful, which brought him pleasure.

When we changed bed linens, Bill helped. Long before I needed the blanket, he started to put it on the bed. This happened repeatedly, and my voice got louder, my tone sharper. (Where was my resolve to adjust my tone?) Again, he chose the blue blanket before sheets were spread. When it was time to get the blue blanket, he didn't understand my asking for it. After we made up the bed, I apologized to Bill for shouting at him, but he'd forgotten. I said, "Thank you." We hugged, and he said, "I like."

6-15-23—Some days would differ from our routine, but then it returned to its previous way. We would then experience a drastic venture into my husband's "toddler stage." This morning he came out of the bathroom and asked me to go with him. To describe the scene in a few words: his bowels had an explosion.

Bill showed me a towel and said something like, "I did not do this." Telling him it was alright, I asked him to leave and I'd take care of it. He headed into the bedroom to change underwear. Remarkably, I remained calm. Putting on disposable rubber gloves, I mopped twice. After about an hour I became satisfied all was clean. Instead of washing old towels and rags I'd used to clean the mess, I tossed them in a sack and threw them into the big trashcan outside.

One night, waiting in bed for Bill to come from the bathroom, I dozed off. When Bill came to the bedroom, I awoke and gave him his bedtime medication, then helping him put on a Depends. I started my shower, but he came to the door twice, smiling and asking if I was coming to bed. I tried to explain what I was doing. Perhaps my having already been in bed caused his confusion. He might have assumed it was later in the night. Who knows? But I vowed not to make that mistake again.

Another afternoon Bill stayed in the bathroom quite a long while. With the door locked, checking on him was not possible. I heard water running in the tub before he opened the door, and he seemed alright. At least, he said so. I picked up wet toilet paper from the tub and threw it away.

Later in the day Bill wore his leather jacket and hat, and he asked if I was ready to go. With a bit of teasing, I stated he wore his winter coat yet it was summertime. He said, "I like it." He kept asking when we were going. I assumed he wanted to go out to eat, but Becky had prepared supper. Even after taking off his coat and hat, he went back to the closet and put on a baseball cap and sweater. Oh, such fun.

7-12-23—I searched for a hand towel usually hung on the loop in the bathroom. I had seen it last night; surely it would show up somewhere. Often we found items out of place, such as his hearing aids, dishes, and clothes. It could either be a nuisance or we found the humor in such oddities. Objects often appeared later on Bill's desk, not their usual place. As for the misplaced hand towel, I kept looking.

I recalled the time Bill wandered around in the living room while I slept through it all. Out-of-place items led me to know something unusual had happened during the night. And his memory didn't function well enough to provide answers and satisfy my curiosity.

7-12-23—My sister Martha wrote with questions about Bill and me. Her interest confirmed my reason for writing this memoir. She asked if Bill was able to take care of his ADL (Activities of Daily Living), and the term came from her job as an occupational therapist assistant. ADL included problems related to hygiene such as brushing teeth, dressing, toileting, taking showers. I could write pages about those issues, because we dealt with challenges daily.

Cleanliness

What frustrated me, what provoked a sour expression on my face, was Bill's complete lack of cleanliness. After he pushed down garbage in the trashcan, he reacted adversely if I told him to wash his hands. Good hygiene had always been Bill's habit. But it was not his priority when the disease took over. When I insisted on a shower, an argument ensued, even though he seemed content after a shower.

As I've said, Bill's aversion to soap became the reason we didn't allow him to wash dishes anymore. He liked being helpful, but we chose to keep him from drying dishes as well as setting the table. He wiped his nose with his hand and onto his jeans as a toddler would. We kept hand sanitizer in the kitchen solely for Bill's use; and he gave no objection about holding out his hand as I squirted sanitizer. In order to remove Bill from the kitchen after a meal, I continued to say, "Let's brush our teeth," and he followed me. Sometimes he would brush his cheeks with his toothbrush, thinking I'd handed him shaving cream.

Getting dressed in the morning, we experienced some silly diversions such as his putting on a pair of my pants or deciding to wear his Sunday best on a Wednesday. So I kept watch on his progress, unwilling to redo his mistakes later, which could cause conflict in us both. His usual response: "This is the way I always do it." My reaction was never pleasant, wanting to finish the process.

Night time usually involved my helping Bill put on a Depends before getting into bed and my adding a clean pad to his underwear ready for the next day. He didn't resist this part of daily care, and I was grateful. If on my trips to the bathroom during the night, I'd find Bill had left a used Depends beside the toilet, I woke him to say, "I'm putting you in clean underwear." Showing it to him, he didn't resist, and even helped. If I chose not to take care of it then, I'd be sorry in the morning when he couldn't get to the bathroom in time. His dribbling on the way to the bathroom during the night had soiled the carpet and we couldn't get the smell out.

Affection

My sister Martha asked if I received hugs and kisses from Bill. Yes, he was affectionate and became the one who first said, "I love you," and then I responded. Bill blew kisses my way, and giving him peppermints made him smile, often with a hug. At bedtime, after leading in prayer, we kissed and I said, "I love you." He usually said "Yes" or "Good." Then "Good night." I cherished Bill's signs of affection. This substantiated what we had read—people with dementia often become more affectionate and express their emotions more.

Bill often acted silly—clucking his tongue, clapping his hands, puckering his lips, marching in place, and teasing me. During some of these times, while I was intent on getting something else done, his mood often helped me respond endearingly to his silly antics.

7-12-23—Music had always been a major part of Bill's life. At an early age, he took piano lessons and loved to play either hymns or classical pieces. However, he now answered "no" when I suggested he play the piano.

He still had a strong baritone voice and followed words on the screen during worship at church. However, he couldn't recognize words correctly if we were singing new songs, Words continued to be more difficult—knowing how to pronounce them or understand their meanings. When playing a music CD at home or in the car, he usually clucked his tongue to the melody. I could tell the tune remained in his memory, as his brain pulled up what notes or melody came next, whether spiritual or classical. The way Bill responded to music brought joy to my heart as well as a smile on his face.

Most important to me: Bill still knew I was his wife. Only once did he act as if I were another woman in bed with him. That awful morning he stood on my side of the bed and shouted, "Get out!" My saying, "I'm your wife," didn't register. He insisted repeatedly I needed to leave, which upset me deeply. Shaken, I got up and left the bedroom. It was early, but I went to Becky's and Paul's bedroom. Knocking on the door, I called to Becky. When she came to the door, I told her, "Your dad has lost it." I explained what happened and how mad her dad appeared, supposing I was another woman. She wisely advised I wait a while, because he might be alright soon. True to form, it didn't take long for him to calm down. By the time we ate breakfast, Bill had forgotten all about the episode and everything went back to our normal.

7-13-23—Becky took a flight to Texas to visit their daughter, Chrissa, and family. While she was away, those weeks amounted to more time for me in the kitchen, including planning, shopping, and cleaning. This meant less time at my desk, while time for Bill's care increased as his needs changed.

I emailed Becky: "Let me sum-up," a phrase captured from *The Princess Bride* film.

"One afternoon I asked if your dad wanted to go downstairs with me. He stood outside the coat closet wearing his leather jacket and hat, saying he was cold. He agreed to trade the coat for a sweater. We went downstairs to make up beds after our family's visit. While Dad stood at the bottom of the stairs, I called to him from the bedroom door. He looked at me, lost his footing, stumbled, and fell backward, knocking down a bamboo room divider. Nothing broke. He said he was okay as he got to his knees and sat on the couch. I made up the beds and we returned upstairs.

"Later as he came from outside, Dad said, 'It's hot out there.' He took off the sweater, but seated in his chair he made a shivering motion. So I handed him a blanket. New every day, even within a day."

Plans changed as Becky wouldn't return from Texas for another two or three weeks. Chrissa and family would be moving to the north side of Indianapolis. So Becky stayed longer to assist with packing and cleaning. What a treat for the family to be closer. Joana was the first grandchild.

Getting Dressed

I sent a quick text to Becky. "Picture this: Dad was in our walk-in closet getting dressed. He pulled his shirt up over his feet. I smiled at this unusual scene as I sat on a chair outside the closet. I didn't correct, because he soon figured out what was wrong."

That day started with Bill being confused, not understanding such words as teeth and pill. Although not unusual, his confusion continued throughout the day. While I began breakfast, Bill first sprinkled my granola on his Cocoa Puffs and then stirred my yogurt and berries, eating from my bowl as he stood at the counter. His actions surprised me, and I reacted abruptly with, "That's mine," and washed the spoon.

7-21-23—Another night we experienced a similar issue with getting dressed for bed. I forgot to hang up a clean nightshirt. He put on one of my shirts. It fit tightly, but he looked satisfied. At first he didn't want to take off my shirt, but I handed him a fresh nightshirt. As I hung up my shirt, Bill put on his T-shirt instead. I persuaded him to take that off and put on his nightshirt. Finally, he was ready for bed.

Due to my unhealthy attitude, I continued to expect Bill to remain the intelligent man I had married and who had a good memory. I wanted him to understand me the first time I said something, so I didn't have to repeat or find different word choices. Unsatisfied, I slowly made progress in this adaptation, and while I had signs of adjusting to hard reality, my reactions were not always healthy for Bill nor me.

After reacting unkindly in what or how I said something, Bill would quickly forget the encounter (an advantage of memory loss). However, I did not easily forgive my shortcomings in thoughts, attitude, and speech. That needed to change, but it must start with the heart and mind before it got out of my mouth. I prayed, "Set a guard over my mouth, LORD" (Psalm 141:3). I pressed on, situation by situation, day after day.

In our study, our desks on opposite walls meant our backs were to each other while he played computer solitaire and I worked on writing projects and added to this memoir. If I turned around when he might seem stumped with a game, I didn't interrupt or fix it. As long as he seemed satisfied, I should be.

Satisfaction was another thread of advice given by our children. As long as their dad remained happy, I should allow him to do whatever he wanted. But I asked myself: Shouldn't there be boundaries? What about my needs and happiness? I struggled with those questions: Was I being selfish or only reasonable?

Our future, though uncertain, would see an increase in Bill's dementia and my continuous learning how to handle our disagreements. Aspects of Bill's progression of the disease began to quicken its pace. My goal remained to show loving kindness to my husband.

Changes and Cleanliness

8-6-23—Changes in caregiving for Bill mostly related to cleanliness. One Sunday while I prepared Keema (an Indian dish of beef and rice), Bill stood in the hall and Paul noticed first that Bill's jeans were wet. I gave instructions to Paul about next steps in the recipe while I headed to the bathroom with Bill. At first he didn't want help, but eventually he allowed me to assist in getting his wet clothes off and into clean ones. He resisted the manner in which I wanted to complete the process. He didn't understand sitting on the toilet when there was no need to use it. But pulling off his jeans while sitting was easier. I brought clean clothes to Bill and put the soiled ones in the laundry.

With that finished, Bill seemed satisfied. He sat at the table ready for dinner to be served. Throughout this process, Paul prepared the Keema, asking me through closed doors only one step in the recipe. I thanked Paul for cooking and his patience with the situation, but he said, "I only helped."

8-7-23—A day later I was confronted with another challenge: a major mess: While cleaning up urine and feces in the bathroom, I told myself, I don't want to do this. Then I quickly added: I don't want anyone else doing this for my husband. I was not ready to move Bill into a memory care unit. I still wanted to care for him, even if it meant messy care. This was my choice and my preference, but I understand it may not be the best choice for others dealing with care of a loved one.

That day's mess counted as the worst Bill ever made, and involved mysteries. I could not understand how his underwear got soiled but his jeans not even wet. Was the heavy amount of fluid on the floor urine or water? I found no evidence Bill ran water from the tub that spilled onto the floor. The toilet seemed to be working properly. No clear answers, but this awful mess took me over an hour to clean.

Throughout the process of cleaning, Bill stood in the hall with a smile on his face and even said, "I like to watch you." The only time he became irritated was when we sat in the walk-in closet to change his clothes. My tone of voice matched his, then I asked him to look at me as I persuaded him to take off his shoes. He finally agreed. I also put a new incontinence pad in his clean underwear.

Questions for Reflection:

1. What are you doing to build up your faith? By yourself and with others?
2. Has it been easy or difficult to keep up spiritual habits: reading the Bible and praying?
3. How has church been a sustainable help during your caregiving?

Photos of Bill and Ann Coker

Bill and Ann on their
50th wedding anniversary, 2007

2nd Christmas in Indianapolis,
2018

Photo of Bill used for books
and podcast

65th wedding anniversary,
Indianapolis

Bill reading his published book in our study

Bill reminding me it's time for lunch

A repeated habit: Bill straightening his desk

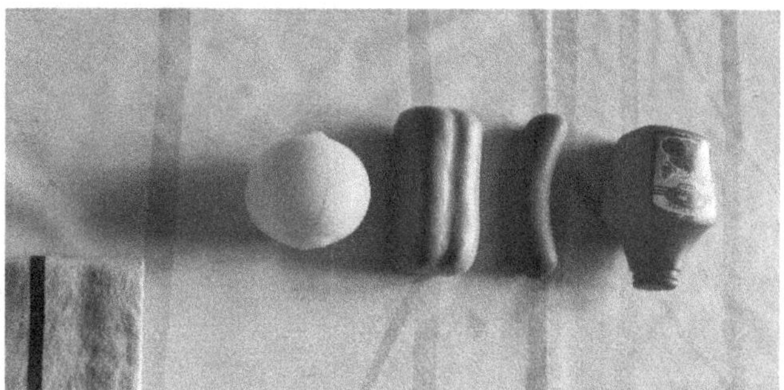

Bill once chose these plastic toy items spread out for his lunch

Framed photo and our motto
from Robert Browning's poem

Early one Sunday morning, ready
for church, avoiding a shower

Bill giving one of his serious talks:
"Do what's right and good"

Gearhart family, Christmas 2023. Paul & Becky are behind Bill & me

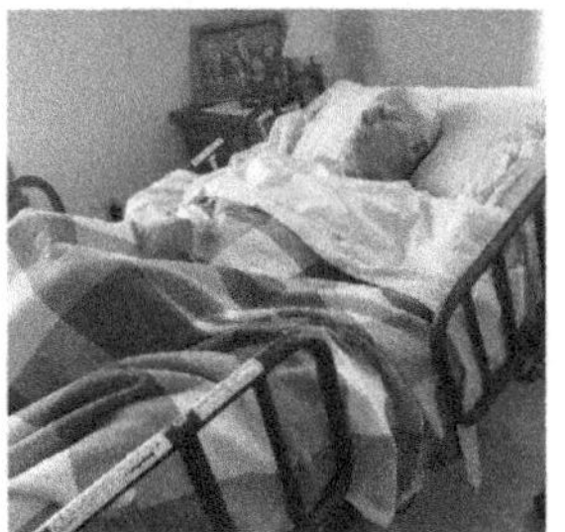

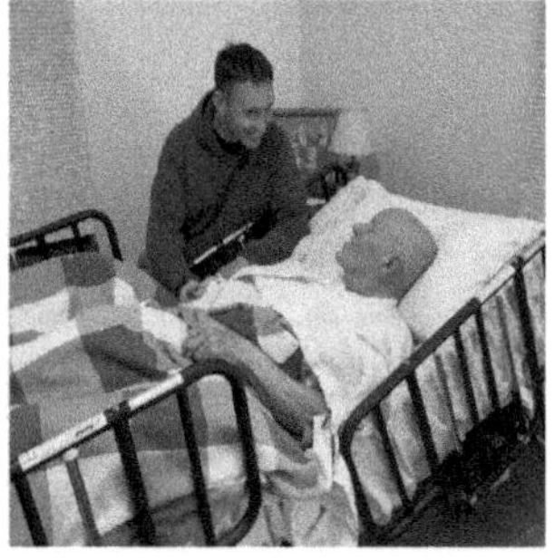

February 2024, Bill in hospital bed.
Framed photo of Coker family

Grandson Wes with Bill, February
2024. On March 7, 2024,
Wes visited us and discovered
his grandpa had quit breathing.
The family gathered by Bill's side.
Becky used her statoscope to listen
to his heart: "He's gone."

Bill did not adjust well to a
wheelchair, February 2024

Gravestone in Terre Haute, IN, shows
dates of birth and death for Bill

Focus on Family

Our family often expressed their perspective about Bill's dementia.

8-14-23—Becky wrote and posted the following on her Facebook page.

"I just had a 20-minute 'conversation' with my dad. I absolutely have *no idea* what he tried to convey. It began with his showing me the two locks on the back door. There was something not right in his mind about the locks, although they both seemed to be working fine. Then he began stringing words together, and in his mind he was making perfect sense. All I could do was listen and nod . . . and try not to cry.

"My dad used to teach a class called The Art of Preaching. He was gifted with teaching and preaching. He loved to read to gain knowledge and as a hobby. Words were extremely important to him. He can no longer read, unless it's put to music, and then he gets most of it right. Now he doesn't usually talk much, but when he does, he can't put together a complete sentence. We often try to figure out what he means and use different words or hand gestures if we want to say something to him, because our words didn't compute.

"Alzheimer's dementia has been slowly taking him farther and farther away. He's still here physically, but my dad is no longer here. It's a slow death and hard to watch up close. But God is still good and His mercies never fail. God is still on the throne and He is still sufficient!"

In July of 2023 our granddaughter, Anna, and her family spent two days with us. The triplets, Ethan, Naomi, and Levi, saw up close what dementia looked like by being around their great-grandpa. Since Anna is a psychiatric nurse, she helped answer the kids' questions to gain good insight. At one point, Anna used her phone to show her kids an image from a CT scan: a healthy brain and a brain affected by dementia. Dark areas represented spaces left absent in one's memory. These images can be also found in literature from Alzheimer's Disease Research.

Since Bill liked to play solitaire on his computer, the triplets joined him, and soon they took over the games, having good fun with their great-grandpa who occasionally instructed them. While giving one of his "talks," Naomi sat near him. Afterward, I asked what they talked about.

She related it was what he used to do and doing it right, his common theme.

While Anna engaged in conversations with her grandpa, she showed more interaction than I had been doing. After one talk, I asked Anna how she involved herself in the conversation. Impressed with her patience and endurance, I gleaned a few pointers. She concentrated on keeping the talk going, whereas I often wanted it to end. Anna repeated some of his words, or gave a sense of agreement and appreciation of what he'd said. I'm certain Bill would have liked that from me also, but it was not an easy lesson to apply. The level of love Anna showed went above her training as a nurse.

Anna later sent a reflection of her grandpa, starting when she was young. I quote:

"My relationship with Grandpa has never been built on a lot of words. It's been the jovial twinkle in his eyes when he looked at me, the instantaneous hug or arm around me when we were close, and the feeling of being loved for who I am. Grandpa has always been special to me for these reasons. I don't think I was 'special' to Grandpa in the sense of being his 'favorite' or anything like that, yet Grandpa had a particular gift for making someone feel seen. The special nicknames, the little jokes, his raised eyebrows with wide eyes, the popping of his denture. Grandpa sought to bring laughter and joy to his grandchildren.

"When Grandpa began the early stage of losing his memory, he forgot my name, and later, he didn't know my relationship to him or even who I am. It's been difficult to watch these slow progressions, yet his good spirit and twinkle in his eyes remained. He still lights up when I or my children enter the room. He still makes those funny faces. Our kids nicknamed him 'silly grandpa' because they have been recipients of his joy.

"When we were together during our last visit (July 2023), I had the honor of sitting with Grandpa during one of his talkative episodes. While we didn't solve the world's problems, or even make a whole sentence, I would like to say I helped him feel seen, as he would do for me. He had something he wanted to say and I listened. I added to his talk to show I could be an active participant in our conversation.

"While Grandpa has long forgotten our conversation (and me), I still remember. Sitting in his presence and seeing the light in his eyes, I 'understood' what he was saying. I loved getting to be that person for a moment. May we always take an extra step to help someone feel seen and heard. The content is irrelevant, the feeling is what lasts a lifetime. That is one of the greatest gifts Grandpa taught me and he never used any words."

Anna's phrase about taking "an extra step to help someone" moved me to think of *The Pilgrim's Progress* by John Bunyan where Pilgrim was stuck in the bog and a person named Help came to get him out. Help asked, "But why did you not look for the steps?" Pilgrim's help was available in the steps that would rescue him. I related this tale in my book, *Journey with Bunyan's Pilgrim*, and added my takeaway: "Asking for help hasn't slowed down my process but instead given answers to speed me on my way."

Ambiguous Loss

In a blog post, I wrote about the term ambiguous loss. It's a term explained by therapist Pauline Boss. The person is physically present but psychologically absent. Becky, in her Facebook post, referred to this by saying her dad was here but not here. While Bill was present, what he was once had now passed away. In his talks, we heard a jumble of words. His sentences no longer made sense, although we liked to figure out what he'd said.

One evening Bill entered the kitchen as Paul and I prepared supper. Bill started to talk with his usual theme of doing what's right and good. We clearly understood that much. His serious expression showed it was important to him.

A few mornings later at two o'clock, I awoke to see Bill standing by the bed and talking with a sense of urgency about what's right. As I stood by his side of the bed, he pointed a finger at me and said, "It would be good for you to do what's right." He continued to talk as I persuaded him to go to the bathroom. As if in a world of his own, he talked in a subconscious state, perhaps similar to a sleepwalker. At breakfast I told Bill he had preached during the night. No response, but it was a fun story.

8-14-23—I read about the topic of peace. One word, *staying*, stuck out because of the need in my life to stay connected to God's peace as I responded to Bill. Tired of the ups and downs, ins and outs, especially my tone of voice which reflected my inner thoughts toward him, I needed the *staying* power of peace. "You will keep in perfect peace those whose minds are steadfast, because they trust in you" (Isaiah 26:3). Trust God; He knows all our needs. As God dominated my thoughts, I *stayed* in His powerful peace.

I prayed: "Hold me, Lord, in Your perfect peace, and *stay* with me moment by moment as I relate to Bill. True peace will be mine when sending my requests to You. Only then will Your peace dwell in me and surpass all understanding. Amen."

More on Cleanliness

To help with cleanliness, I placed a small rag towel on the floor in front of the toilet (to catch drips), but I kept finding it in various places: on the side of the toilet, on the counter, even in the tub. While at first I explained to Bill the purpose of the towel, that was useless. My attempt to keep the bathroom clean did not connect with his limited understanding.

I changed hand towels when: Bill wiped his face on the one in the kitchen, or (excuse the honesty) when he had used a towel in the bathroom after having a BM. The latter was disgusting to me, but correcting Bill didn't work well. He had forgotten and I couldn't change his actions.

Convincing Bill to take a shower always proved to be a challenge. With my slightest persuasion or loudest argument he refused and told me he didn't need to bathe. I could not change his will. He put up strong resistance with his facial and verbal expressions. There were no good explanations why he avoided a shower; it wasn't likely about fear of falling. More reasonable: his logic and understanding were nearly absent. The steps involved in the bathing process were perhaps too difficult and he refused help.

How I reacted to Bill's reluctance (downright refusal) depended on several matters. I may be tired, or I'd had a frustrating day dealing with Bill's confused state and was unable to get much writing work completed. As this continued—my efforts to persuade and his insistence to do as he pleased—I wanted to call it quits. Each of us got louder, back and forth, and he usually won, much to my dismay.

I evaluated why cleanliness mattered so much to me. Bill used to love taking showers, sometimes two a day if he'd been working outdoors. His current resistance was definitely "not Bill." I wanted to reclaim who he used to be, but that was impossible. Was my insistence on cleanliness related to good health? Probably not. Was my desire that he shower on Saturday night so people at church wouldn't be offended? Could they perhaps smell an odor? More likely, it corresponded to me, my reputation, and not about Bill. I'd come to the crux of the matter. Me and my way.

Words Lost in Meaning

Bill enjoyed helping me with the mail. He would bring my letters out to the mailbox, but he started to forget to put up the red flag. I began to put any outgoing mail in the box, but Bill continued to retrieve the mail. He liked sorting mail for Gearharts and for us. He smiled and read aloud his name on envelopes, even the junk mail. One afternoon with hand signals pointing out to the front of the yard, Bill indicated he wanted to get the mail. He asked me to go with him. Holding hands, we walked together down the driveway to the mailbox. Two young bikers passed by and waved. What were they saying about this old couple holding hands?

Generally one of the first indicators of dementia is forgetting names of items and people. Six years after his diagnosis of Alzheimer's disease by the neurologist in Indianapolis, more and more words were lost in meaning to Bill. In the kitchen I wadded up an empty chip bag and Bill held out his hand. I said, "Put this in the trashcan," but I later found it on the counter. The blank look on his face told me he had no clue what I'd said. I repeated it a few times and used hand signals that usually worked.

If I asked Bill to go to the bathroom before we left on errands, I ended up saying pot instead of toilet, but I often needed to point. Once after asking Bill to go to the bathroom, he headed to the bedroom closet before I stopped him.

As we returned from the grocery, we each held bags. Stopping by the refrigerator in the garage, I asked Bill to put the milk on a shelf. He had a blank look, and my repeating the request wasn't helpful. So I did what I asked of him. Surprised, he said, "Oh." He may understand once but not another time. Later as I went into the study to say lunch was ready, I repeated it twice and finally moved my hand to my mouth. He then followed me.

Understanding words and their meanings had escaped his mental capacity. This did not represent the intellect of a man with instant recall of words and their significance while teaching and preaching during several decades. People had often praised his vast vocabulary and good syntax.

8-21-23—Lately, Bill would often giggle. This didn't always match the situation. He smiled and giggled when he couldn't recall what to say—unable to find words in the forefront of his mind. Trying to sort out what he was thinking proved a waste of time, even though I made an attempt. Bill's dementia began with loss of memory about people, events, and places, then grew to a lack of connecting spoken words and their meanings.

Some expressions, however, connected readily with their meanings. More quickly than me, Bill became the one who said, "I love you." He expressed his love several times a day. But he also told the dog, "I love you." Using motions connected with his use of "love," he blew kisses or strutted into a room with a smile on his face. My happy camper.

Riding in the car delighted Bill, and he asked most days where we were going, indicating he was ready for an outing, a change in his routine, so I'd drive out into the country. He appreciated houses with land around them, a reversal of shot-gun houses he lived in during his childhood in New Orleans. As we rode around the city, he repeatedly said, "Look," usually referring to the heavy traffic.

8-30-23—Bill slept late this morning and gave me a chance to write a letter to one of my sisters and prepare breakfast without a rush. Our sleeping habits had changed over these years. It was usually 11:00 PM when we were in bed and 8:00 AM when we arose. My bathroom visits during the night were generally once or twice, and uncertain how many Bill took.

Of late I wanted to be up when he got out of bed in order to put him in a fresh Depends, especially if he'd taken off the one he started with at bedtime. I was grateful he didn't resist my help. His wearing one throughout the night varied; so I looked on the bathroom floor for one or noticed if he was still wearing one. It's not something I could depend on (pun intended), and not predictable. When I woke during the night also became unpredictable.

An interrupted sleep pattern became the norm. I'm not a light sleeper, and could not anticipate Bill's nighttime antics. Getting my rest affected whether I woke during the night or convinced (deceived) myself not to be up when he returned from the bathroom. My deprived sleep hit me mid-afternoon while I read or wrote at the computer. Yet Bill took naps in his chair throughout the day.

9-5-23—Bill had forgotten names of family members, even our daughter Becky. When she wanted her dad to bring me something, she said, "Bring this to your wife," and he did. The few times when she referred to me as her mother, Bill didn't understand. When we received cards from our sons, I'd identify a sender as "our son Tom," and Bill's facial expression showed he made no connection. Sometimes showing him a photo helped with recognition.

The main reason for Bill's anger resulted from my making commands. My telling him what to do was usually when he said, "No!" Thus, he let me know he's in the right; it should be done his way. I witnessed this when we got ready for bed. He wanted to keep on his socks or undershirt, as he said it's his usual way. Those times I wanted my way, and I let him know. Pausing to think before I spoke meant I wouldn't be upset later when reflecting how I handled the situation.

One morning Bill opened several drawers in the kitchen. I asked him why, and he turned and stroked his cheeks. Evidently he was looking for his razor. I said it was in the bathroom, but he chose to eat breakfast first. Later in the day he again asked for his razor, stroking his cheeks as an indicator. Another time we found him with a kitchen knife scrubbing it against his cheeks to shave, so we decided to hide the knives. He was happy when I shaved him, and he also liked my putting aftershave on his cheeks. This we soon adopted as a habit.

Once after we brushed our teeth, I left the bathroom. When I returned, Bill was using the electric razor, but it wasn't running. He didn't push the button to turn it on. This time it needed to be re-charged which he didn't understand. On closer observation, dry toothpaste covered his cheeks. I wet the hand towel and cleaned the toothpaste off his cheeks. His sour expression showed he didn't like it. I plugged in the razor to recharge and promised he could shave later.

Allowing Bill to do what made him happy suited him, but I wanted to add limits. Acceptance meant I had to change my attitude about Bill's continuous habits of obsessive behavior. This was no easy adjustment, as you see the ups and downs of my reactions.

The Flood

9-6-23—I awoke at 6 o'clock this morning, and stepped off the carpet on my side of the bed. My feet in slippers splashed into a flood of water. I soon heard water coming from the toilet which was still running. I stopped the flow of water, but later didn't recall the process (which might have been helpful). Jiggling the lever before taking off the tank top, I pulled up the stopper. The latter only increased the water flow, so I pushed the stopper back down. I began some clean-up, pulling up small rugs and sloshing them into a bucket to carry out to the sink in the garage.

Knowing I couldn't handle the large rugs, now heavy with water, I waited an hour to call Paul. Willingly, he got a wagon to hold the large rugs, and we mopped up water with old towels. Next he was concerned with securing fans to dry his previous work of added sub-flooring. Through it all, Bill slept and snored.

In the bathroom I found only the outer layer of Bill's disposable underwear. I surmised Bill had flushed the inside material of his brief. However, Paul said it didn't explain why the toilet kept running. The inner workings of the toilet could be faulty, and my jiggling the handle stopped the flow.

I could have played the "what if game." If I had gotten up earlier, could I have stopped the flood? But when I did wake up, Paul helped, knowing how to dry out the flooring.

You see, Paul had stripped off most of the carpet in the hall and bedroom, preparing to add a new water-proof flooring. Ironic. The sub-flooring was now saturated from this morning's incident.

Because the flood compromised the sub-flooring, Paul now needed to buy and lay plywood as an in-between solution before laying the vinyl flooring. Getting a new floor installed happened in stages. The main reason: Paul could only work on the flooring during his days off, combined with other household and yard work. The timing confused Bill. He looked at the sub-flooring and tried to pick up what appeared to be white paint splotches. Every day he questioned in such a way that it was evident he didn't understand the process. I added too many details, but then changed to, "We're getting a new floor and it takes time."

9-9-23—This morning when Bill woke up around 8:30, he was very confused, reciting places and names and incidents like he was still dreaming. He also started toward the kitchen before he got dressed, but then followed me into the walk-in closet where I had his clothes ready. I repeated requests that he take off his soaked Depends, which he finally did. Now he could dress himself while I finished breakfast preparation. Returning to check, I noticed he patted his back pocket, wanting his wallet which we hadn't located in several days.

It was Saturday and college football games played on TV. Tulane played Ole Miss. Although Bill's eyes were closed, he said, "I'm listening." I commented a few times about the score while he smiled with some indication of what transpired. College games were once his favorite Saturday pastime, and he often added loud commentary. Now it only seemed to help as a distraction from naps.

9-13-23 –Bill stuffed a new area rug into the trashcan next to his desk. Earlier he had looked at the two rugs on a chair near his desk. I hadn't decided yet where to store them for use on the new flooring in our bedroom. When I asked him to hand the rug to me, he refused until I said "please." This was one of those times I didn't let him do what made him happy.

I remembered an incident in November of 2021. Around 2 o'clock that morning, I awoke to a commotion, things bumping and moving. I saw Bill in front of the bedroom window, and he was putting my house shoes and socks onto the sewing machine. I got up as he was putting the wicker trashcan on top of the sewing machine and it contained his slippers. The little chair nearby had been moved to the hall on the opposite side of a bookcase. Handing Bill his slippers, I asked him to go to the bathroom. He answered, "If that's what you want me to do." After returning items to their proper place, I waited until Bill came back before going to bed.

Those episodes are different from his obsession to shave several times a day. Like yesterday, Bill must have gone into the bathroom six or eight times, only to use his electric razor repeatedly. Because that made him happy, I didn't stop him.

Going into the kitchen to prepare lunch, I noticed Bill at the center island watching Becky prepare a baking order. I asked if she had a new sous-chef. "No," she said, "he's more like a puppy. He followed me into my bedroom as I took off my shoes." Bill often added to our amusement. Of course, Becky would have shut the door if she had gone into her bathroom so he wouldn't follow her.

Later in the day while walking through our living room, I found one of the bolster pillows out of its crocheted cover. Bill, probably bored while watching a western on TV, unzipped the cover to see what was inside.

9-14-23—Today a crew came to install a new roof on the house. The noise at first bothered Bill, but he became more upset with the mess on the lawn and the multiple vehicles parked out front. What disturbed him the most involved the dog. Jules wasn't allowed outside without someone with her. Bill wanted to let her out, and I explained it would not be good because the backyard gate might be open. Bill ignored this as he headed to the back door to let Jules out. I had to intervene.

After lunch Bill stood by the kitchen center island, raising his hand, wanting to touch recipe items Becky had laid out. This created a problem, because of his lack of cleanliness around baked goods Becky would be selling. Finally, Becky said in a soft voice to us both, "It's time you left the kitchen." I agreed. This became a source of anxiety, as Becky had to guard any food or even surfaces from her dad's desire to touch everything with his unclean hands. Food items had to be hidden, everything put away, surfaces cleaned repeatedly.

Needed Advice

9-26-23—This morning I stripped linens from our bed. Three days in a row I had washed sheets and remade the bed. I didn't wake up when Bill took off his Depends or stood by the bed, wetting rug and floor. I remembered God's words, "and your strength will equal your days" (Deuteronomy 33:25). I had applied this promise caring for our children when they were little, and I needed it now with changes due to Bill's dementia.

Was there any way to prevent the necessity of washing sheets as an oft-repeated routine? I phoned Aleen. Her suggestions varied: order adult diapers; either sit up when Bill went to the bathroom (and stay awake) or follow him; and in due time, I might want a porta potty by his side of the bed with a covered trashcan nearby. I searched online and found a few good products. That night I combined two brands (Depends and pad) until the order arrived later in the week.

No need to wash sheets the next morning—a nice relief! The doubled nightwear briefs worked to keep Bill and the bed linens dry. When my order of nightwear arrived, I became convinced they would not work, designed as a wrap instead of a pull-up. I planned to shop and buy adult diapers.

I did research, found, and purchased a bed alarm online. After it arrived, I read the instructions twice, needing to be confident how to use it. The foot mat meant the monitor set off a chime when Bill got out of bed. There would be no problem about my going back to sleep while he was in the bathroom. The foot mat and monitor alerted me when he got back into bed.

9-29-23—This morning Bill acted as if he had lost his voice. Still in his nightshirt, he sat on the edge of the bed and I asked kindly if he would like to get up. He made no movement but looked at me with a blank stare. To my questions he offered no answers with no hint of anything wrong. This continued several minutes as I encouraged him to speak. Nothing. Worried his voice had gone, my chest tightened. A line from *Jesus Loves Me* came to me with a bit of change: "I am weak, but He is strong." Eventually

Bill said something without much meaning and stood up. Was he just being stubborn?

In our office another day, I turned from my computer and noticed Bill slipping down in his chair. I said, "Bill, please stand up." He didn't. I explained he needed to sit straight in his chair. He remained seated and grinned. Was this stubbornness again? It was difficult enough to adjust to his dementia; stubbornness would be an unwelcome addition.

9-30-23—Cleanliness continued to be a major issue. After using the toilet, Bill would sometimes swish his hand inside the toilet to wipe away feces. Of course, when present, I made sure he washed his hands. But would he have washed if I were not in the bathroom? Not likely. This added to Becky's anxiety about her dad in the kitchen.

One Saturday night I wasn't sure what finally convinced him to shower, but he took off his nightshirt and moved toward the tub ready with mat, soap, and washcloth. After a short time, I helped him out of the tub to dry off. Using this time to compliment him, I mentioned how clean he looked and how he always liked hot water. He smiled and said, "Thank you."

10-1-23—Sunday morning I tapped off the alarm clock and turned back to sleep. Waking up later than planned, we had less time before leaving for church. I decided we'd get a doughnut and coffee at church. At the serving table before Sunday school, I asked Bill to choose which doughnut he wanted. He pointed to two. While talking with Paul, I turned away and Paul said Bill fingered other donuts. Actually he had leaned on the table to steady himself, but he had touched the display of sweets. Embarrassed, I led him toward the classroom and returned to get our coffee.

We had been attending a Sunday school class using the book *The Gift of Empathy*: *Helping Others Feel Valued, Cared for, and Understood* by Joel P. Bretscher and Kenneth C. Haugk. The chapters emphasized methods of empathy with various age groups. I'd been able to relate experiences with parents, siblings, and friends. The chapter dealing with empathy toward a spouse helped me better understand the need to express empathy toward Bill during those times when he showed disappointment with his own actions. As I listened to Bill and understood dementia better, I could be patient with his efforts to express himself and his need to be helpful.

Mentally I applied the gift of empathy as I imagined myself in Bill's situation. What must it be like to deal with incontinence? Again, that associated with the disease and not him. Wanting Bill to know I understood his needs, I could show him I cared and not be judgmental or expecting him to react properly. Bill was my husband no matter how he behaved, and I loved him. As I gave expression of my love, he would know. My discomfort with Bill's changes should be faced honestly and not evaded.

During the class discussion, Bill scratched at spots on the table. Nothing removed the spots, but he continued. Later during the sermon, Bill dozed or at best would nod. I held his cold hand and roused him to sit up straight. It was still worth the effort. How would I know when it became futile?

First Sunday of each month they served communion at church. As our row arrived at the front of the sanctuary where servers held the elements, Bill motioned me to go ahead of him. I helped Bill with the elements. One usher held the tray of bread cubes in little plastic cups; another usher had the grape juice. Each server showed thoughtfulness in presenting the elements.

Bill fingered several cups of bread before I chose one for him. He held it until I took the bread out of the cup and put it in front of his mouth. The same with the juice. He started to put his cups back in the tray, but I retrieved them to place in the basket held by the third server. We headed back to our seats while I considered the many times Bill administered the Lord's Supper at churches and Emmaus gatherings. He was known to give brief but meaningful messages before communion. People often asked him to officiate, and it became his signature service. Now he didn't know what to do with the elements. His behavior became childlike, and I was disappointed. On the way home, neither of us made conversation.

10-4-23—Reading from *Daily Creative* today, Todd Henry advised writers to start with the impossible and the practical will follow. Being a caregiver made a good application. It's impossible to be perfect at this task: to make choices throughout the day; to have Bill as he had been before dementia set in; to work well together with family. Because this caregiving task seemed almost impossible, I needed to work toward the goal of what's practical, to accept what I'd been given. As I cleaned Bill, his clothes and the floor after an accident, I admitted it was unpleasant at best, ugly and filthy at worst. I compared this grown man's debilitated state with a child's oft-repeated accidents.

When our children were infants, my caring tasks seemed natural, but with their dad, my husband, it was unlikely I'd gladly accept these tasks as part of my given role. This difficult acceptance turned practical on a daily basis when I acted out of necessity, taking care of him willingly, even those times when it was not easy. I acted out of love for my husband, because God gave me the privilege to care for Bill.

10-9-23—Tonight Bill dressed for bed in his nightshirt. A few moments later Bill put his blue jeans back on with his nightshirt tucked in. A funny sight. After some persuasion, he took off his jeans. He insisted (in his usual explanation), "I always do this."

I slept later each morning, because of interruptions during the night, such as putting another Depends on Bill. Another morning Bill had no desire to get out of bed. Urging him numerous times, I heard him insist he was cold. Probably because earlier I had mistakenly yanked the covers toward my side of the bed, sending cold air his way. He was not out of bed until 10:00 AM and we ate breakfast at 10:30. Soon Bill pointed to the clock, ready for lunch. Noon on the clock meant lunch ought to be in process. Repeating my adjusted time frame didn't suit him.

10-10-23—Our pastor friend, Paul Z., phoned to check on us. It'd been his routine to call and we liked his attention. After giving him a quick update on Bill's progression, Paul recounted being one of the clergy on a recent men's Emmaus Walk. The clergy team included Gary S. and Howard H., and they expressed appreciation about Bill's commitment to the El Shaddai Emmaus community. Bill's clergy talks became their own. Paul reported that people probably mentioned Bill a dozen times during the weekend. These spiritual retreats had comprised a large portion of Bill's time and energy, but he loved the opportunity to expand his ministry into the community, outside his local church. Bill's influence continued with appreciation from team members.

10-17-23—We had to laugh: Becky found her pumpkin-shaped cookie cutter in the dog's toy basket. Much to Becky's chagrin, Bill had a habit of picking up Jules's toys off the floor and putting them on the kitchen counter. Playing opposites in Bill's head: he took cookie cutter from kitchen counter to put in dog's toy basket and dog's toys onto the kitchen counter.

Continued Incontinence

10-18-23—Bill's incontinence issues became more time-consuming. With accidents during the day and night, it meant changes of clothes and washing bed sheets more often. When an accident happened, he came and said, "water." We headed to the walk-in closet to change clothes. At nighttime the bed alarm alerted me when Bill got out of bed. I stayed awake while

he went to the bathroom and returned. Only once did he get upset—when I tried to take off a wet Depends as he sat on the toilet. After resisting my help, he finally yelled, "Get out!" which I did.

Thinking back on that incident, I would approach it differently next time—without commands that possibly made him feel ashamed, and my appeals to logic which were now impossible to interpret. Becky reminded me of the difference between talking with young children and someone with dementia. A child is in the process of learning. Her dad was unlearning skills. He no longer had the ability to use logic, but relied only on his stubborn will to get his own way.

Caregiving involves both mental and physical abilities. Mentally, I learned how to approach Bill and relate to his personhood, respecting who he had been and who he had become. Physically, the time required for his care mostly dealt with his incontinence. The bed alarm, even with its good points, meant more interrupted sleep for us both. Either we needed to go to bed earlier or accept these late times of starting the day.

Talking with Becky was always helpful, and I admitted that I expected more of her dad than what's realistic. My expectations were formed by the Bill I once knew, not who he had become. Becky asked if we owned long-term care insurance. We did not. She reminded me that memory care units are expensive. Someone suggested we take advantage of adult day care centers, where we could bring Bill for the day. Although some folks would find that valuable, we agreed Bill was too self-aware at this stage, and would probably become angry if we left him somewhere during the day.

10-21-23—I awoke after several interruptions during the night. The floor mat and alarm were working well. If I fell back to sleep while Bill stayed in the bathroom, at least the alarm woke me when he returned. This morning I recalled our children's time in diapers. Long ago we used cloth diapers and rubber pants. Rubber or plastic pants would be helpful to pull over Bill's nighttime adult diapers.

At a home health supply store, I found rubber pants. I also bought adult diapers, but after using them two nights, they were little better than my make-shift Depends doubled with an off-brand. At least last night Bill only wet the newly purchased water-proof mat on top of the bottom sheet which stayed dry. Getting more waterproof mats would prevent having to wash sheets every day.

10-24-23—When I told Bill to go to the bathroom before we left on errands and before going to the dinner table, it was like persuading a child. My command expanded, because he often didn't know what I requested. Such as one day, when we returned from lunch at McDonald's, I said, "Use the pot." I pointed to his crotch and then to the toilet. He stayed there an extra-long time, and I opened the door to ask if he was okay. He nodded.

After he came out, I said he needed to brush his teeth. As he stood in front of the sink with his toothbrush, he unbuttoned the top of his shirt. I pointed to his mouth, and he understood. Later I found his electric razor wrapped in the hand towel left on the counter. Another unsolved mystery.

Questions for Reflection:

1. How have family members viewed your caregiving? Supportive or not?
2. I explained "ambiguous loss." How have you dealt with the away but present in the relationship with your loved one? Does this make sense to you?
3. Have you been given good advice and encouragement from your family?

Facing my Faults

Becky and I read the following helpful advice online. While they are good instruction, we found it not often easy to practice.

"Living with Dementia."

1. Agree, never argue.
2. Divert, never reason.
3. Distract, never shame.
4. Reassure, never lecture.
5. Reminisce, never say "remember."
6. Repeat, never say "I told you."
7. Never say "you can't."
8. Ask, never demand.
9. Encourage, never condescend.
10. Reinforce, never force.

I would add:

11. Say "Let's go." Never "Go."
12. Use positive words. Never say "Don't. Stop. No. Not good."

Consider the second instruction, (2) divert, never reason. With Bill's reasoning ability non-existent, it became useless to appeal to logic. I remembered not to say "remember," and instead brought up stories from the past as a way to connect and reminisce. One of the hardest suggestions was number (8) "ask, never demand." While telling Bill what I wanted him to do, I didn't say he "can't," but my asking seemed more like a command. Paul and Becky would remind me to say "please." Cooper E., a teen boy at church, said it well in his message one Youth Sunday: "Negative action doesn't need negative reaction."

10-25-23—As Becky prepared supper, her dad continued to touch items on the counter. In frustration, she tossed something behind her back. I asked what it was. She said, "Eggshell." I reminded her of when we had only been here a few weeks and I had told Paul, "This is no experiment. We are here to stay." Becky said, "This is all on me." She was frustrated but not angry. Yes, each of us became weary of Bill's antics, but we would either put up with it or laugh together. This path meant attributing these difficulties to the disease. Responses from Becky and Paul reassured me, and they helped to dismiss my thoughts about our being a burden.

Routine Mattered

10-26-23—The notion of routine mattered to me but not to Bill. Every night his denture needed to be soaked and cleaned, but most nights, he objected. I held out the container and asked for his denture, but he didn't understand. I tried different terms: denture, upper plate, or false teeth. He wouldn't release it, and repeatedly said, "No."

With the task undone I left the bathroom. When I returned Bill still wore his denture and had filled the container with water. If he put his denture in the cup, he might squirt lots of aqua-colored toothpaste in it. That seemed wasteful to me, but not a bad option to Bill. My only solution? Be content and wait for my opportunity later.

10-28-23—While I talked with Amazon on my phone, Bill stomped his feet. I turned around as he pointed to the clock on the wall. 12 noon. We had eaten breakfast three hours ago. I turned back around only to hear him beg my attention again. This we repeated three times until I completed my call, and he was happy when I started preparing lunch. Again I adhered to his wishes, thinking of what our sons advised repeatedly: "Whatever made Dad happy." I asked myself: Is there no reverse strategy? When it was time to move into Daylight Savings Time, Becky teasingly suggested I move the clock time forward so it would be 1:00

when her dad pointed out it was noon. Might this be dishonest?

10-30-23—One night I dozed briefly while Bill was in the bathroom. I woke knowing he had not returned. Checking, I found him on the toilet holding a small towel, and on the floor I saw a pile of inside material from his Depends. He motioned to the floor that I should pick up all the diaper's innards. When I wiped Bill's hands, my concern level rose. I saw dried blood on his left hand. Further investigation found blood on his nightshirt. During the night he evidently scratched a hang mole on his chest, causing it to bleed. Still unconcerned, Bill only wanted the floor clean.

After he calmed, he allowed me to wipe off the blood and change his underwear and nightshirt. Finally we returned to bed. I spotted some blood on the top sheet, but chose to take care of it in the morning. I later shared the incident with Becky.

10-31-23—I told Bill breakfast was ready, left him in the bedroom, and soon returned to find him in front of his computer, swiping the computer mouse around his cheeks. This was after he had used the electric razor in the bathroom. A video of this would have been proof of his funny antics.

When talking with Bill, I had weak persuasive power. One morning I said he needed to take a shower because of our appointment with the dermatologist and our annual scans. As I prepared the tub and gave Bill reasons to have his skin clean, his answer remained, "No," as he pointed his finger at me. After several attempts and his refusals, I conceded. My only alternative would be to sponge bathe him before we left for the doctor's office.

11-1-23—Another late start to a day, and I was partially at fault. Not wanting to get up, I questioned what prevented me. Not ready to face the Zoom call scheduled to market my book; not wanting to deal with caregiving; not willing to take care of myself as I ought (exercise and eat healthy)? God's mercy persuaded me out of bed, knowing He is always willing and able to meet my every need and to forgive any shortcomings during the day.

Disagreements

Again Bill disagreed with my invitation to get out of bed. By 11 o'clock he went into the bathroom, and I'd already eaten breakfast. He came to ask help with his belt. He still wore his nightshirt, so we returned to the walk-in closet to change clothes. Breakfast ended at noon, but at one o'clock, he let me know lunch should be ready. He wasn't satisfied as I explained breakfast had only been an hour ago. I sliced an apple and brought it to his desk. We ate lunch around 2:30, a bowl of Becky's good beef and barley vegetable soup from last night. I anticipated Bill would point to the clock again at 6 o'clock.

While in the kitchen one evening, Becky came to say her dad had picked up and bitten off the point of a purple marker. She told him it wasn't candy, but he aimed a disgruntled facial expression at her. I brought his bowl of ice-cream, saying, "This ought to taste better than the marker." His lips and mouth were purple.

11-3-23—I had to pay constant attention to Bill at church during the preaching—persuading him to keep his eyes open. One Sunday Bill almost fell off his chair. It startled a friend sitting behind us as she gasped and I smiled. Later I told Becky, "You say *my* job at church is to keep your dad from falling off his chair when he dozes off." She agreed. I continued, "*Your* job is to keep me from killing your dad." Today was one of those days. I recalled how Ruth Graham responded in an interview about her husband Billy. Did she ever consider divorce? Her answer: "Divorce? No. Murder? Yes."

I understood, especially during Bill's arguments as he shouted, "No!" and pointed at me to leave a room. Lately it had happened more frequently. One afternoon we were standing in our office, and I don't recall what started the argument, but Bill got very angry. My mistake was not overlooking it. I obviously said something that irritated him, and he raised his voice, raised his arm, and looked as if he wanted to hit me. That was a first! Surprised that he might actually want to hurt me, I began to cry and left the room.

Another time, when Bill was getting dressed, the pad in Bill's underwear slipped out of place, hanging out to the side. I asked him to pull down his underwear so I could put the pad back in place. He didn't and repeated, "No!" I said, "Look down at your leg and you can see the pad." Again, "No!" I tried to explain, but he would not listen and shouted, "Go! Get out!" Offended, I raised my hand toward him but retrieved it quickly. Bill repeated, "Get out!" and I left. When he took off his underwear that night, the pad was still dislodged from its natural place.

Repeatedly in the bathroom I'd hear Bill shout, "No! Get out!" It happened when I wanted to clean him with a disposable warm cloth. In a disagreeable mood, he wanted to be in control. After all, he was an adult, even if he acted like a toddler. Most of the time he would win the argument while I left in disgust. Not a pleasant ending, much like a mother, upset with a disagreeable toddler.

11-5-23—One of the most frustrating (and unreasonable) aspects of caregiving was caused by my inability to learn a lesson well enough to make it stick. I was like a teenager caught between childhood and adulthood. One moment I would change my attitude in the way I responded to Bill, and the next moment I'd revert to a condescending tone in my voice. I wanted Bill to know I understood his behavior, but I failed to communicate, and I was left discouraged.

Thankfully I learned from God's word. Today's verse on my phone's Bible app read: "You are the light of the world" (Matthew 5:14). The speaker emphasized this wonderful responsibility we have to be light in the darkness, as he recited ordinary ways to practice this privilege. One example given: show kindness to store clerks and neighbors. Being kind meant being light in the darkness. Wow, that struck me between my heart and mind! When being kind to Bill, I could be light that reflects Jesus to him and to others around me. I asked myself: will this lesson stick? How long before I'd forget and return to my poor tone of voice? Belittling Bill added to the darkness in our little corner of the world.

Another verse on the Bible app connected with being light: "Let your conversation be always full of grace, seasoned with salt" (Colossians 4:6). My reactions toward Bill needed to be altered—be gracious, seasoned with salt which preserves and adds a pleasant flavor.

11-6-23—Bill woke up around 5:00 AM. He had wet the bed, so I turned off the bed monitor and followed him into the bathroom with a clean night-shirt. I asked him to take off his nightshirt (not to his liking), and I returned to the bedroom to check on the bed linens. Shocked, I found *all* the linens, including the top comforter, soaked with urine.

Telling myself I had always liked the chore of making a bed, I stripped the bed and began putting on fresh linens, getting different blankets down from a shelf in the walk-in closet. Back in the bathroom, Bill didn't want me to use a warm wet disposable cloth. He wanted it dry. So I placed the cloth and towel next to him and returned to finish in the bedroom, finding the floor also wet in places. I mentally thanked Paul for completing the new vinyl flooring that replaced the carpet. Paul's reason: "It smelled better." Yes, also easier to clean and keep dry.

I consulted with Becky about what to do better, how her dad could stay dry during the night. I already used the best of adult diapers. Less liquid intake before bedtime, yes. She suggested whenever I'm up at night, I wake her dad, especially when he didn't go on his own. Since I did not go in the bathroom with Bill, I also could not confirm if he had emptied his bladder. The monitor alerted me when Bill got up, and I could add waking him during my times to the bathroom. Sounded like a good method.

11-7-23—The next morning we awoke to a dry bed, proving once again we cannot anticipate what one day will be, compared to the latter. My one attempt that Bill follow me wasn't successful. I had nudged Bill on the shoulder, and asked him to go to the bathroom with me, and while he startled awake, he quickly fell back to sleep.

Reaction vs. Response

Consider the difference between reaction and response. "To react is to operate purely on instinct. To respond is to listen to your instincts but pause and allow wisdom and experience to guide your actions. When we respond rather than react, we are far more likely to make wise choices and far less likely to cause ourselves trouble down the line" (*Daily Creative*, Todd Henry). I could prevent my reaction to Bill's dementia by pausing, praying, and responding in wisdom. Often when I responded well, Bill acted chipper and would say, "I like it."

11-12-23—At church this Sunday we ate pancakes during community hour—a fundraiser for the junior high youth. In line Bill remained quiet. We sat at a table and a friend joined us, engaging Bill by asking about his previous ministry. Bill began to talk, and even though it didn't make much sense due to broken sentences, our friend nodded in agreement. This kept Bill talking, and I appreciated our friend's support.

A few mornings later Bill uttered a complete, understandable sentence with noun and verb in the right position. This happened again a couple of days later. These were rare occasions at this stage of his dementia.

11-14-23—Even though Bill had not put the red flag up on the mailbox lately, I requested, "Please take these letters to the mailbox and put up the red flag." Looking out the window, I saw he did not complete my request. I walked to the mailbox, but didn't find my letters there. I looked in our study and kitchen. No mail. I went out again through the garage, looking to my right and my left, and I discovered the mail in an unlikely place: on the seat of Paul's motorcycle.

11-18-23—It was 12:30 PM and Bill reminded me it was lunch time. We had eaten breakfast late again. Going into the kitchen later, a strange sight awaited me on the table. Lined above Bill's place setting were several plastic food items designed for a child's toy kitchen—a lemon, a hotdog in a bun, and a bottle of ketchup. I asked Bill if he put them there. "No." But Paul had earlier seen Bill arrange them. On Facebook Messenger, I sent a photo to our sons with the caption, "Dad's choice for lunch." John asked, "What's with Dad's plastic diet?"

11-25-23—Tonight I lost my temper and my opportunity. Bill put on his nightshirt and together we went to the bathroom. Since it was Saturday, Bill should take a shower and be clean for church tomorrow. Reacting to my request, he shouted, "No," and didn't budge in the direction of the tub. Skipping his Saturday night haircut was not a good choice on my part. Continued persuasion led to shaming him: "It's been a week since you bathed and now you stink." Bill said, "Now listen!" I interrupted saying, "No, you listen to me. You need to bathe." He refused again. I opened the door and we both left. I'd blown it big time! I had yelled, insulted him, and all the while used disrespectful words. It ended with him having his way.

Still upset, I cried out to God. "You know I'm tired of this—acting well, and then doing poorly—in and out of emotional stress." It's like the classic story by Joel Chandler Harris, told by Uncle Remus about Br'er Rabbit and the Tar-Baby. The more Rabbit fought, the more entangled he got in the tar. My tactics were wrong, and I needed to change the Saturday routine to one that worked: start by cutting Bill's hair, and then he would shower without an argument. Washed in God's forgiveness again, I took my shower. In bed, I prayed out loud and kissed Bill good night. Forgetting about the incident, Bill smiled as I said, "I choose to love you." Yes, it's a choice, plain and simple.

11-26-23—The Sunday after Thanksgiving we watched football games into the evening, and we ate supper seated on the couch in the family room. About 9 o'clock, I went into the kitchen and Bill followed me. I said, "You can start getting ready for bed." While he was in the bathroom, I pulled down the covers on the bed. Bill walked into the bedroom, and I motioned to the walk-in closet and said, "You can undress now." He gave a quizzical look and said, "No. I need someone who knows." I said, "I'm someone who knows." This we repeated a minute or so while I said it's bedtime. Bill continually refused to undress, even after sitting on the cedar chest in the walk-in closet.

I said, "Take off your shoes," as he pressed his feet against the floor, not allowing any help. Again he repeated, "I need someone who knows," so I said, "I'll get Becky, our daughter." She stood in the closet doorway and said, "It's time for bed." She asked if he wanted to take a shower. I teased, "You're pushing it now." Bill didn't make a move while I held his nightshirt. After Becky left, Bill began to take off his shoes. I opened the hallway door to thank Becky, "Your dad has put on his nightshirt and gone into the bathroom."

11-27-23—After lunch Bill came out of the bathroom, and his face had splotches of blood. I was curious what caused the blood, knowing the electric razor never cuts him. He followed me, and I washed his face, applying two bandages where blood still seeped. Because he had previously taken off bandages, I asked him to keep these on. He nodded. I never found out what caused the blood.

12-6-23—Early during the night hours I headed to the bathroom. When I returned to bed, Bill giggled and clucked his tongue. A bit irritated, I said, "Be quiet." He asked, "What?" I repeated my request, and he stopped. Guilt filled my mind, and I recalled the definition of love in Paul's letter to the Corinthians. First, "be kind," but "irritable" better described my behavior. Yes, love meant being kind—even in the wee hours of the night. Love gives meaning to life.

Bill's silly antics lasted into the next morning. He awoke with a smile, and at the breakfast table, he teased me. The day was pleasant, one with Bill's humor in top form.

12-8-23—Bill developed a few favorite words for numerous occasions. "Really" was the word he used most often. If asking him to come and brush his teeth or follow me to the bedroom, he generally asked, "Really?" If saying, "That's your iced tea," he replied, "Really." The word didn't contribute significantly to the conversation, but it became his way of saying something, even if oft repeated.

Grateful for Little Things

Bringing joy to my heart, I would count how grateful I've been for the little things Bill still remembered and connected to our routine. Music topped my list. Bill recognized a melody, even though he no longer sang the words, he recalled the tune. He hummed or clucked his tongue, ready with the next chord or verse. He often slapped his knees or clapped his hands together. I've said of Bill, "Once a drummer, always a drummer." That began in grade school when he played drums in their little band in New Orleans. He's never owned a set of drums, but he's a drummer at heart, easily recognizing rhythm and beat.

In a framed photo in the hallway showed Bill and our grandson, Michael, when he was three years old. With knees slightly bent, they both patted a tune with hands on their thighs. Later Michael played drums in high school, in church at the contemporary service, and even taught lessons to a few young men. I'm grateful music still appeared as deposits in Bill's memory bank.

I was also grateful for Bill's continued demonstrations of affection. He would often blow kisses and request hugs. His sense of humor brought much joy—even though I didn't always appreciate his comedic timing, such as when I was in a hurry. I was glad of Bill's kind disposition. Even when I became abrasive, he didn't usually react with anger. Thankfully, in those times when I spoke ill toward him, he would quickly forget whatever offense took place. More often than not he had a pleasant expression on his face.

When Bill saw my name on an envelope of incoming mail, he would hand the letter to me with a smile. While he no longer called me by name, he often expressed his love in words and action. Also Bill still lifted up the toilet lid and seat, then closed it after use. While not a big issue, I was thankful for such little things.

12-13-23—We continued to connect with people from our former churches. Two friends visited to buy Bill's books. I met them at the front door with hugs as they mentioned, "We pray for you and Bill." Both are retired medical workers: John K. a pharmacist and his wife, Connie, a hospital nurse. We shared a nice chat. They appreciated what I'd written in our Christmas letter, and showed empathy about our caregiving situation. Bill spoke only a half-dozen words after my asking him to keep his eyes open. We talked about our attending church here, and they encouraged us to continue as a witness to others. Church members here in Indianapolis had also expressed something similar.

Some Sundays, I asked myself: Was it worth the effort? For quite some time Bill hadn't participated in Sunday school or worship. How long would we continue this ritual? Although not ready to quit church attendance, how would I know when we needed to stay home? Should we continue for *my* sake or would it become too difficult?

Even though his lifelong ministry centered around church, it seemed Bill gained little from the habit of attendance. By this time, he had quit singing during worship. However, he continued to interact with people, especially children, as we moved about in the hallways. He appeared to enjoy being in church. After all, church had been part of who he was.

Getting Bill ready for bed did not become a chore until he decided it wasn't time. The process took various forms, unpredictable and lacking understanding. Sitting next to him, he may ask my help. If I put clothes in the hamper and returned, he might be pulling his T-shirt over his nightshirt or he hadn't put on slippers as he normally did.

Before getting into bed most nights, I'd ask Bill one last time if he wanted to go to the bathroom. His usual reply, "A little." The amount of time he stayed in the bathroom could be weighed against time saved in the morning. During cooler nights, Bill rarely got up. His wetting the adult diaper proved to be no problem to him. He was kept warm.

Wearing rubber pants over his Depends soon became a bone of contention. Two nights in a row, skipping one night, and then the fourth night, he started to take off the rubber pants while in bed. Around midnight each time, I sensed his movements. If I stopped his actions, he'd agree to keep it on. But one night I got agitated when he took it off the third time. I tossed it behind me into the corner of the room. He went into the bathroom, and when he returned I put the rubber pants back on him. He did not resist.

One night Bill started talking. I couldn't tell if he was asleep or awake. Although I drifted off, I soon sensed Bill taking off the rubber pants again. In a loud voice I said, "Those need to stay on all night. They keep you and the bed dry." He alternated between pulling down the pants and allowing me to reposition them. Again I became frustrated about the ordeal. "Now go back to sleep. And quit talking."

The next night Bill headed to the bathroom before daylight. I checked the bed pad and it was dry, and he'd not taken off his nighttime briefs. When up in the morning—the pad, sheets, and nightshirt were all dry (of course, not his brief).

A good start to the day, but I couldn't depend on that happening each morning.

12-14-23—I had a new question for the pharmacist. Bill started chewing his pills before swallowing them, and on occasion he spit out a capsule after chewing it a while. I needed to know if this was a problem and if he was getting the proper dosage. The pharmacist looked at Bill's list of medications, and he suggested giving Bill the capsule at a different time of day; so that he might swallow it whole. The pharmacist also assured me chewing the tablets together should not make a difference. We tried to follow the pharmacist's advice.

12-15-23—I reported to Becky about her dad's accidents and changes. Each day proved different. One night he took his cholesterol medication at bedtime, swallowing it without hesitation. Another night he spit it out. The pill possibly tasted bitter the longer it was kept in his mouth. I questioned if this medicine was still necessary. I wanted to follow the doctor's order and reasoned that without the medication, he might have a stroke.

Wandering Inside

We kept aware of where Bill wandered around the house. When he left our office, I checked where he went. I was mostly concerned because of his lack of cleanliness. He touched everything, especially in the kitchen.

Letting the dog outside, Bill may stop in the kitchen to watch Becky cook, and too often he interfered with her process. While Becky baked, she or I watched her dad. One day he stuck his hand in the large open bag of flour on the counter; another time, in a large bag of shredded cheese. We didn't know if his hands were clean, so this posed a problem.

One afternoon Becky caught her dad looking at the partially completed jigsaw puzzle on a table in the family room. She asked him to move away and not to touch the pieces. He shouted, "No!" Not convincing her dad after several tries, Becky turned off the overhead light. Bill left the room. The puzzle was one Paul ordered and upon arrival he found the pieces very small and each piece similar in shape. Paul stated it had not been a fun puzzle to put together, yet he accepted the challenge to complete it. If Bill took apart what had been connected, it would be quite frustrating—perhaps to the point of throwing away the puzzle.

12-21-23—One afternoon before leaving to the post office, Bill motioned me to come into the bathroom where he pointed to the floor and a pile of feces. After ushering Bill into the bedroom closet, I handed him clean clothes. Staring first at the mess in the bathroom, I questioned what would be the most sanitary way to clean. After putting on disposable gloves, I chose a disinfectant, old towels, and plastic bags.

Cleaning and disposing of everything hadn't taken much time, and after mopping the floor and Bill changing into clean clothes, we headed to the post office. Throughout the episode, Bill remained calm and I was grateful he accepted my help.

12-23-23—The Gearharts celebrated Christmas on Saturday before the holiday on Monday. We took turns with in-laws and scheduled our time when family members could travel. Traditions included large handmade stockings stuffed with wrapped gifts in various shapes. Bill paid little attention to his own gifts but liked watching others unwrap theirs. Becky served a delicious meal with dessert choices. This pleased Bill who took a bit of each sweet.

Christmas Eve we attended the early contemporary worship service at church. Back at home, Bill and I sat in the family room and gazed at the brightly decorated tree, a special tradition we enjoyed sharing with family.

12-28-23—Each morning one of several options greeted me. Either Bill slept during the entire night, waking wet or dry, or he got up once or twice. I wasn't sure which I liked. If the bed linens remained dry, that option was preferred. One night, however, Bill stayed in the bathroom longer than usual, and I discovered the delay. He had locked the bathroom, so I used a small screwdriver to open the door. Upon entering, I saw a few small white paper-like specks on the floor, and Bill motioned me to pick them up. He'd taken apart the inside materials of his nighttime brief and deposited the shredded parts in a basket next to the toilet. At least he'd not put those in the toilet as he did months prior when we experienced flooded floors. Asking Bill why he'd done this would not reveal any information. He would have no explanation or it would be forgotten.

Bill was dozing throughout the day more often, either in front of his computer with a solitaire game on the screen or while in front of the TV. Should I have asked him to pay attention? Did it matter? While at the computer, he dropped the mouse control from his resting hand on the desk when he dozed off, and I lost count how often this occurred during a day. Facing my computer and with my back to him, I didn't see it, but would hear it drop to the floor. Once Bill held the mouse at the top of the computer screen and pushed buttons trying to start a game. His confusion could often be amusing.

Mealtimes proved a similar challenge. Should I correct his table manners? Before we were all seated, Bill might reach a portion from one of the serving bowls, and I often stopped him. If he used his fingers to pick up cooked vegetables, it wouldn't be kind to tell Bill he's an adult and should use his fork. At the end of the meal he would pick up his plate and lick it. While this became his usual habit at home, at a restaurant I removed his plate before he could lick it.

Once after supper, Paul and Becky noticed Bill look at me and raise his eyebrows several times. Paul made a cute remark about our getting ready for something later, but Becky added, "He'll forget it in five minutes."

Bill frequently had a runny nose. Giving him a tissue and saying, "Your nose is running," didn't always lead to expected results. If I wiped his nose, it was treating him like a child. Was this important? Again it indicated to me the constant issue of expectations versus reality and what was necessary.

Over and over I said to myself, "I'm tired." This was emotional, not physical. Weary of this caregiving, I too often interacted unkindly toward my husband who could not understand simple directions. I was weary of the frequent changes in routine. While I admitted being tired, I chose not to relinquish my caregiving responsibilities to anyone else, even a medical staff person. Choosing to be my husband's caregiver, I accepted this not only as my responsibility but my privilege. Other caregivers may choose out-of-home care, and that may be their best choice. We all need to consider the positive and negative aspects of our particular situations. Every situation and every person is different. We had the advantage of living with our daughter who is a registered nurse.

My choosing to speak negative words, such as "stop" or "don't" or "no," only aggravates someone with dementia. But Bill's ready use of "no" while pointing his finger made it difficult to react well. Before considering my options, my initial reaction was often rude. I slowly learned how to communicate in a kind way toward the man I loved.

Most of my fears were linked to the future and how I adjusted to Bill's progression with dementia. In my routine I neglected consistently needed exercise for my arthritis. I took my medications and applied creams. While helpful, it wasn't enough. Not walking properly with my back straight created problems, I started using a cane to help with my posture and balance. Would I be physically ready when Bill needed me the most?

Questions for Reflection:

1. I confessed my faults and failings in caregiving. How are you dealing with those?

2. What routines and habits have you found unnecessary and even harmful?
3. Could you relate to the difference between reaction and response? How?

PART III

____

The Ending—
When It Turned

I found myself separating days between living in the valley or on the plain, both with their challenges. More often than not it became difficult to persuade Bill to do what he needed. He had lost the ability to understand explanations, and questions confused him, even simple ones such as: "Where did you find that? Or where did you put your wallet or hearing aids?" He had also forgotten names of most items or where they were generally kept. These mountains became more difficult to climb.

Our kids encouraged me to "let go" regarding changes I experienced with their dad. I worked daily toward putting their advice into practice. One morning Bill made up the bed without my help. Tempted to re-make it "better," I left it alone.

However, holding back from expressing something out loud did not mean victory. My thoughts indicated true feelings.

One morning I didn't criticize Bill when a puddle appeared in the bathroom, rugs were wet, and his nightshirt was damp and wadded up on the counter. Upset anyway, I had not truly let it go. My inner disappointment and weariness existed even when I didn't verbalize my feelings. I washed the rugs, his nightshirts, and a towel on Saturday, while Becky teased me, since my laundry day had always been Friday.

In the process of helping Bill one night, he gently shoved me aside. I let him have his way, not correcting him on the spot, but it hurt my feelings. Later I asked him not to be rough with me. But, of course, he had already forgotten the incident. When I asked about two missing items, he didn't respond. I found them later. Paul had moved one and the other Bill had put in the trashcan. While responding better with patience, I still could not control Bill.

1-1-24—Holidays and special days on the calendar became meaningless to Bill. Christmas came and passed, and he paid little attention to either the house décor or the Christmas lights outside. On Sunday, New Year's Eve, we stayed home from church because I had a sore throat, but not attending church went unnoticed to Bill, only he stayed in bed longer. We watched the church's worship service online. I should say, I watched while Bill sat nearby, awake but with his eyes closed. New Year's Day we had no special plans, but he did ask where we were going. This time he expressed no disappointment when I answered, "We're not going anyplace." He returned to his computer solitaire, and later he watched football bowl games on TV with the family.

Challenges Increased

When getting dressed and undressed, both morning and evening, the challenges and changes significantly increased. One morning he put on his shoes before pulling up his jeans. He became upset when I wanted him to take off a shoe; he didn't notice both legs were not yet in his jeans. After showing him the problem, he relinquished control and took off his shoe. Sadly I watched his memory fail him with simple tasks. These learned tasks he forgot at a rate I wasn't ready to accept.

1-2-24—This morning started like many others by getting up late. At 8:45 I asked Bill to join me in the bathroom. I handed him his underwear as he sat on the toilet still wearing his nighttime diaper. The odor alerted me he'd had a bowel movement, and I asked him to stand up and take off the underwear. As he stood, the mess increased. After some clean-up, I turned on the water in the tub and told Bill he needed to bathe. Not surprisingly, an argument started.

As he backed up to the tub, his idea was to sit on the side and wash himself. The more I insisted he bathe, the more he resisted. "Get out," he said. I asked him to look at me as I tried to reason with him, saying "please." He yelled, "I know what I want." Again he shouted, "Get out!" With a huff, I left.

When I returned, he had washed and dried himself without a shower. I helped him into clean daytime underwear and onto his feet. Smiling, he said, "Thank you." By the time he came into the bedroom to get dressed, he'd forgotten about our argument and harsh words, and he asked me to button his shirt. With breakfast at 10:15, we could start the day, late again.

1-8-24—To minimize Bill's angry outbursts, I phoned his neurologist and asked for an increase in his anti-depressant prescription. Becky agreed this was necessary. The suggestion to double the dosage continued for a week, and I called the doctor back to report the results. I did not like Bill's response. He became more lethargic, dozing more during the day, and it seemed his confusion also increased. Yet he still slept well during the night.

The next two days I divided the dosage between morning and evening and saw some improvement. His neurologist sent in a new prescription, but given at bedtime didn't work well either. I preferred dealing with his occasional tantrums, and telling me "no" when I asked him to do something. We eventually chose the twice daily dosage of his previous anti-depressant.

I continued to use the one accepted procedure to deal with incontinence. Instead of a pad in his cotton underwear, I added a pad inside a Depends and he wore that during the day. I introduced it with no explanation, and Bill didn't question the change. These got discarded at the end of the day, almost as soaked as his underwear had been. Would this change be disagreeable to Bill? Thankfully it was not.

The issue of incontinence during the night remained unsolved. With a pad in overnight briefs (Depends) and rubber pants, most mornings he woke with soaked briefs and a damp nightshirt. I hadn't found a suitable combination to keep him fully dry, even if he went to the bathroom during the night. Using a waterproof pad on the bed helped to keep sheets dry most nights. With four sets of bed pads and rubber pants, it still meant extra laundry during the week. One morning Bill woke at 7:00 o'clock and the bed alarm alerted me. When he returned to the bedroom, he entered our walk-in closet, leaving his wet articles in the bathroom.

Another morning he awakened drenched in urine, but he refused to shower after my attempt to convince him it would be good for warm water to run over his body. Instead, he wiped himself with a hand towel and put on his underwear. Even though I had changed bed sheets the day prior, I needed to change sheets again. Laundry had never been my dreaded chore, but now the reason became a stickler.

Incontinence and cleanliness were still the most unpleasant areas of caregiving, and perhaps as you read this you are tired of my repetition. The way I handled these areas affected the difference in my attitude. Sometimes it involved tricks and treats: I tricked Bill not to handle items with unclean hands by changing his focus; and then offered a treat when he became compliant. Often a peppermint or a kiss on his cheek.

1-13-24—Bill often expressed thanks. While I prepared our lunch, he stood by the counter to watch. When I handed him his plate, he beamed and said, "I like that" or "good." He'd never been one to give compliments on food. Instead he would say, "It's okay," when asked if he liked something. With breakfast he might pause eating his Cocoa

Puffs and say, "I like this." Most of the time, he just ate, without a word.

Useless Explanations

1-19-24—Last night I described as "rough." It began as we were getting ready for bed. We had watched reruns on TV, and I told Bill it was bedtime. After taking my medication in the kitchen, I went to pull down the covers on the bed. I asked Bill if he needed the bathroom or was he ready to undress. He smoothed down his shirt, indicating he wasn't changing. I insisted and even pulled up the shade to show darkness outside. Not convinced, he stood outside the closet and casually watched me put on my nightgown.

Bill then sat on the cedar chest as I helped take off his shoes. I told him to take off his shirt. "No!" he yelled. "Not what I do!" Keeping calm, I explained his disease kept him from knowing what he needed to do. Choosing to explain made no sense, because he had little reasoning capabilities. He finally took off his shirt and jeans but not his socks or underwear. His insistence increased along with his shouting. After I went to the bathroom and returned, he still sat in the closet. I got into bed.

He soon came to bed carrying a pair of my dress pants. I shouted, "Those are mine!" He threw them at me and returned to the closet. He chose a flannel shirt and pulled on a different pair of my pants. Going to the closet and taking those away, I handed him a pair of his sweatpants and returned to bed. With his daytime Depends still on, he put the nighttime adult brief on top and then the sweatpants, keeping on his socks. Between two and three o'clock in the morning, he had pulled off the sweatpants. Around five o'clock he got up, went to the bathroom and returned.

The next night proved to be a similar process, so I asked Becky to talk to her dad. Bill met us in our hall and motioned he did not want to return to our bedroom. Becky took another approach and said, "Okay you don't need to go to bed." She headed into our living room and turned on a lamp, inviting her dad to sit on our double recliner. He seemed satisfied. She returned to the family room as I prepared for bed. I kept the light on in our walk-in closet, and around midnight Bill came into the bedroom, turned off the light and got in bed fully dressed. I said, "Good night."

The End Began

1-20-24—About mid-morning Becky met me in our office and gave her medical advice regarding her dad and me. She made several points. First, I needed to relinquish my rigid schedule and face the fact my husband would not improve. Second, we would change his wardrobe from jeans to sweatpants with elastic, allowing more flexibility and comfort. If he chose to sleep in those clothes, let him. This clothing would also help to clean him if he wet himself. Third, we would eliminate all his meds except the anti-depressant prescribed by his neurologist. With medical facts, Becky backed up her recommendations. The dementia medications had become ineffective during this advanced stage of Bill's mental decline, his brain having lost most of its logic and understanding. His other prescriptions and supplements were not necessary as he neared the close of life. For example, he did not need the medication to lower his cholesterol, and he argued about taking it anyway. The double dose of anti-depressant made him more compliant at bedtimes. Getting him out of bed in the morning still challenged me, but I also slept later.

I emailed the new changes to our sons and received their responses by email, text, or phone. Bill Jr.'s reply supported our decisions and added that I needed to care for myself. John and Tom agreed with their sister about withholding prescriptions and supplements. John backed it up with a medical report, and reminded me we had legally declared Becky as our advisor for medical decisions.

It became time to allow Bill's condition to progress naturally as he would have desired. While a difficult decision to carry through, I admitted Becky recognized what was best for both of us. Hardships are our counselors, and each hardship came with a dividend. But it's up to us to collect it.

I phoned Bill's doctors (PCP, urologist, neurologist), leaving messages about our decision to eliminate medications except for the anti-depressant given twice a day. Nurses called back, and I explained our decision. The neurologist's nurse sent a revised prescription to the drugstore. The urologist's nurse took notes and requested we contact them if Bill developed any urinary problems. The urologist had already addressed Bill's incontinence.

1-21-24—The next night combined not letting go of my rigid routine, Bill dealing with my demands, and an instant answer to prayer. We started getting ready for bed. When he exited the bathroom he wore only his T-shirt and long-sleeve shirt. Mistakenly I had already laid out clothes in the closet for the next day, and he started to put those on. At first he chose to wear the corduroy pants, pointing his finger at me and shouting "No! This is what I want!" I kissed him. He calmed down and gave me the pants. Next he held his nightshirt and shoved his leg in at the neckline. I explained he was doing it the wrong way. He got it up to his belly but no further. After I left for a minute and returned, he'd taken off the nightshirt. Holding it, he wouldn't accept my request to pull it over his head.

I closed my eyes and briefly prayed out loud. I asked God to help each of us get ready for bed, to be calm, and do what was right. When I opened my eyes, Bill was pulling the nightshirt over his head. Why didn't I pray earlier when the conversation had been more heated? Yes, "the one who is patient calms a quarrel" (Proverbs 15:18). The rest of the routine went well. Another decision made: wait until morning to lay out Bill's clothes for the day.

The following day Aleen visited after Becky had informed her about our changes. Aleen's experience with adult daycare enhanced her knowledge and compassion. With Bill in the room, we talked about him and she agreed with changes in his medications and wardrobe. Wearing sweatpants did not become a challenge like I assumed. Aleen said staff of nursing homes advised families to bring in loose-fitting clothes for their patients. I told Aleen I had adopted my goal for the new year as "patient endurance." She said I should call it perseverance.

1-23-24—Our son John drove to Mobile, Alabama, to attend the funeral of my sister Minnie's husband who died of Parkinson's disease. Within a two-year period both my sisters became widows.

My sister Martha's husband died in January of 2022 from Covid with health complications. I assumed my husband would soon follow.

1-28-24—Sunday morning I again turned off the alarm and slept almost another hour, which meant we only attended worship and not Sunday school. Bill wore his new navy sweatpants, a dress shirt, and a warm vest. The advantages: no bothering with a belt for dress pants, and when we returned home he had only to change out of his dress shirt and into a sweatshirt.

Sunday evening proved to be challenging, because we dealt again with Sundowner's Syndrome. Bill was not ready for bed at our usual time. He changed clothes but started to pull up the covers on his side of the bed. My voice was not gentle; I expected him to obey my wishes. I even prayed to be kind, knowing it was the answer to my prayer. Once I calmed down, Bill got into bed. But he didn't understand that he needed to move closer to the center of the bed. Too close to the edge meant he might fall. I repeated to myself: I am not giving up.

Part of the night Bill slept on his right side, facing the window. In the morning his nightshirt was wet, and he allowed me to help him dress for the day. He put his sweatshirt on backwards, but gave no resistance to changing it. Getting into his new

Sketchers slip-on shoes became easier for us both. I was grateful we had a good start to the day.

The next night went smoother as we prepared for bed. Bill also went to the bathroom without my invitation. Returning to bed, the process declined. He took off the rubber pants and threw them into the trashcan near the window. He wouldn't cooperate with my putting on a new pair for the rest of the night. The morning started well, but after breakfast he had wet his sweatpants and T-shirt. I helped him change. Around 11:30 he turned away from his computer and asked what we were going to do. Although bored, he would have to wait a while to have lunch.

Reading my Bible, a verse in Isaiah caught my attention: "people whose speech is obscure, whose language is strange and incomprehensible" (33:19). That phrase described Bill's speech, because he stammered, and we didn't understand most of what he said. However, he repeatedly spoke of doing what's right and good. I found that phrase in the apostle Peter's first epistle. "For it is God's will that by doing good you should silence the ignorant talk of foolish people" (2:15), and ". . . do what is right and do not give way to fear" (3:6). When we do what is right, the good follows.

2-2-24—Bill no longer played solitaire on his computer. When I showed him how to move cards around for Spider solitaire, Bill pointed to cards, but he wouldn't use the mouse control. The game's rules escaped his understanding. He'd gone from playing three different solitaire games to one (Spider) and now none. In the past this took up a good bit of his time, so now we needed to look for something else. He often organized and re-organized items on and in his desk, but that wasn't always productive. I removed the tape dispenser because he took it apart and couldn't put it back together. He had also lost meanings of objects, even pens, a coaster, and a tablet of paper.

To occupy his time, Bill began to look through large books we kept on the coffee table. First, he thumbed through the two about pregnancy and childbirth. Then I handed him the book about New Zealand and showed him our friend Stefanie's photo, because she lived and taught in New Zealand. Next he looked through a large book about hummingbirds, and he thumbed through the artist Kincaid's book. He seemed satisfied with these photo books. He picked up a family photo album Becky had prepared several years ago, but he didn't view it at any length.

Becky assured me her dad was now in the advanced stage of Alzheimer's, and not because we withheld his two prescriptions for dementia. This advanced stage usually progresses quicker than the moderate stage he's been in for over eight years.

Explaining to friends about withholding Bill's medications evoked different responses. One friend at church looked alarmed, although she didn't voice her objection. Another friend gave an understanding nod we were doing what's right; she had cared for her mother during dementia. We shared common experiences.

I phoned the mail delivery service that delivered most of Bill's prescriptions and requested they not automatically send prescription refills. They had mailed one he no longer took, and it couldn't be returned. No charge, however. At least a pharmacy nearby displayed a bin for disposal of unused medications.

Questions for Reflection:

1. What challenges increased for you and in your caregiving?
2. Were there simple or drastic changes indicating your loved one's life was ending?

Facing Fear
of the Future

Seated in the exam chair at the podiatrist's office, I looked across at Bill sitting in a corner chair. He had dozed off, dropped his hands outside the arms of the chair, and woke up with a start. He wore a green plaid shirt tucked into grey sweatpants, making him look puffy and pitiful. Sadly, some people measure quantity and quality of life, and they consider euthanasia advisable for the elderly no longer functioning properly. Most would agree Bill now exhibited little quality of life. When we were ready to leave, the nurse helped me persuade Bill to move out of the chair so we could head home.

Walking to the car, Bill became unsteady on his feet. He had had several falls lately, usually when he stepped backwards. We tried to teach him to use a walker, but he picked it up and held it in the air while slowly shuffling. Also while using a walker Bill would bump into the furniture.

We had a home visit with a nurse, an annually scheduled event by our insurance company. We had been seen by the same nurse the previous year. She noted numerous changes in our health, especially concerning Bill. These she reported to our primary care physician.

During conversations, Bill made no logical sense. He would start a discourse at odd times, as if he'd been thinking of something important and needed to let us know. Because his talks were long, drawn-out, and confusing, it was easy to get impatient. Our desire, however, was to understand each other. Becky would illustrate that my expectations were "here," with her hand held horizontally above her head, and reality was "here," holding her hand at waste level. And then she would say all the space in between was where frustrations arose. I still needed to adjust.

Order Became Absent

2-4-24—Driving from church that Sunday, I mentally rehearsed how we had spent time during the worship service. My attention focused on Bill to keep him from dozing. With all Bill's changes, I was the one who needed to adjust to help order and peace reign in our lives. I resisted change due to pride. I desired order, understanding, routine, and even obedience.

Getting ready for morning and bedtime continued to be the two specific times we faced the greatest resistance. Not only on Bill's part, but mine as well. When he didn't act the way I wanted, I pressed against his resistance. He argued against what needed to be done mornings and evenings, and my tone of voice wasn't always gentle. I continued to insist, and he continued to resist. This revealed the core of his being—authoritative—and my corrections wrestled with his core. He often yelled or pointed his finger saying, "No!" or "Get out!" On occasion he punched his fist in the air as if he would hit me (which he never did).

2-10-24—My friend Donna Dene E. visited and we went out for lunch. Bill stayed home with Becky. Returning, I learned Bill had fallen in Becky's bedroom after he brought her one of the dog's toys. She assisted him up. At night I gave Bill a haircut, but I didn't insist he take a shower.

Sunday morning we attended worship at church, and afterward we met Becky and Paul at China Garden for lunch. Following my usual practice, I ordered for Bill and he enjoyed my choice. During our meal, I watched him closely in case he tried to drink the eggroll sauce or use his fingers to eat. He tried both. I decided this would be the last time we would eat together at a restaurant.

2-16-24—At 7 PM I entered our living room to tell Bill supper was ready. He arrived in the kitchen, carrying two pillows from the sofa. Moving toward him, I grabbed the pillows and it startled him. He fell backward and hit hard. With Becky nearby, she asked him to move onto his knees, but he only wanted to sit up and stay on the floor, saying, "Now listen." Bill touched his elbow several times, so Becky pulled up his sleeve to find he had a gash on his elbow. With gauze, a large bandage, and tape, she dressed the wound. Bill did not attempt to get onto his knees, even when Becky demonstrated what she was asking him to do. She did not want to try to lift him up and injure herself.

Becky and I sat at the table and started eating our supper, leaving Bill on the floor by the doorway, hoping he would be able to follow instructions after a few moments. Soon Becky remembered that Tom P. was upstairs in the loft and she called him to come help. Tom was a strong 26-year-old friend staying with us temporarily. He bent down behind Bill, pulled him up to a standing position, held him to make sure he was steady, and led him to the table so he could eat supper. We appreciated Tom's help, his strength and youth. By the time Bill finished supper, we headed to bed.

Resistance and arguments occurred again as I directed Bill to change his clothes. He didn't understand what he needed to do. I repeated simple instructions, such as taking off his slippers and getting into bed, but he failed to comply. What finally triggered his mind to cooperate was a mystery. Perhaps he was tired, but he finally got into bed. I pulled up the covers to provide warmth, since he was always sensitive to cold.

2-17-24—Saturday morning we were out of bed at the same time and headed to the bathroom together. He did not move toward the toilet or allow me to take off his overnight briefs. After some time, I called Becky to come help. Returning, I told Bill again to use the toilet, and his hand closed tightly over his briefs. Because Depends have convenient sides to rip off with little effort, I did that. He still wore the rubber pants, now below his knees, and he wouldn't pull them off.

When Becky arrived, she asked what I would like to do next. I said, "Pull the rubber pants up so he can walk." This done, he became more aggressive, striking out verbally and physically toward Becky and me. Would he hit Becky? By the look on her face she wasn't afraid. Bill didn't budge. Becky and I left when he yelled, "Get out!"

Paul had removed the bathroom lock, but Bill stood up against the door to block my entrance. In our office I read a short while until Bill opened the door. He followed me into the bedroom but wouldn't go inside the closet. I pointed to his clothes on the cedar chest, and after quite a while he entered but refused again to take off the rubber pants. Eventually, after my leaving him for short periods, he cooperated and got dressed. It was Saturday so I phoned the answering service of the neurologist and requested a call back. It resulted in adding another anti-depressant to his current medications.

Difficult Decisions

I made two important decisions. We would not attend worship service at church the following Sunday and continue to stay home on Sunday mornings unless the situation improved. This was a big decision. Also I would not request Bill to shower, not being confident in his ability to maneuver in the bathtub without falling. My sister Minnie had introduced me to Scrubzz rinse-free bath sponges, which I used before Bill's bedtime, without any resistance on his part.

2-17-24—Saturday evening I called Bill to supper. Becky and Paul had gone out to eat and celebrate their daughter-in-law Emily's birthday with her family. Bill entered the kitchen and with hand signals indicated he had to go to the bathroom. After setting our meal on the table, I left the kitchen to check on Bill. He stood between the sink and toilet, and I was unable to determine whether he had finished. Also he wasn't answering any of my questions. Nothing proved effective, even my giving options about what he wanted to do next: stay there, come to supper, or even go to bed early. Unsteady on his feet, he acted befuddled and foggy. Perhaps increasing the anti-depressant medication had been a mistake.

A physical struggle ensued as I urged Bill out of the bathroom. In the hall, he turned toward the bedroom but refused to move. He bent his knees. Knowing it wasn't wise either to keep holding him up or to release my grip, I needed help. Grabbing the phone from my pocket, I texted Becky and Paul, "Come home." Reflecting later, I should not have alarmed them, and my brief text did not give any understanding as to the critical situation. With some effort I placed a chair behind Bill, but he refused to sit. Acting out of frustration, I attempted to pull him down onto the chair. Understandably, he reacted violently! Thrashing his arms about, he fell onto the floor with his head against the hall door.

Once again I called upstairs to our guest Tom who came readily as I moved the chair out of the way. Tom talked gently to Bill, getting him in a seated position, and telling him to rest a while. Then Tom stood behind Bill and lifted him onto his feet. We both recognized he wasn't steady, so Tom asked where I wanted Bill to go. "To bed." I held Bill's hand and Tom steadied him as we moved slowly to Bill's side of the bed and I pulled down the covers. Tom lifted Bill onto the bed as I took off his shoes. I covered him, and we left the room.

Thanking Tom, I added, "You would work well in a nursing home. I could not have cared for Bill if you had not been available." Becky texted, asking more clarification and I replied, "Dad is now in bed." When they arrived home, we stood in the hallway and I apologized for texting them. I related what happened, which led to a brief discussion about how we needed to proceed. Bill's Alzheimer's had shifted quickly downhill in his advanced stage, and we examined our options to make life easier for him and for us as caregivers. Becky, Paul and I discussed the situation—what would be the best next steps.

We reviewed several options. (1) Borrow a small wheelchair, a hospital bed, and continue his at-home care. (2) Add a senior-care professional to help during part of the day. (3) Admit Bill to a memory care unit in an assisted living facility. Without concern for cost, we set out to research. I openly admitted the best thing would be that Bill be with Jesus. Becky added she had been praying for that, and assured me it wasn't wrong to have those thoughts. First step: Paul would borrow a wheelchair from church the next day.

2-18-24—Youth Sunday we watched the worship service online. I thanked God that Bill had not fallen all day. In the evening we watched a DVD film in our living room. I decided we'd go to bed early, and briefly went to the kitchen. When I returned, Bill fell as he got up from our double recliner. Becky came and used her arm strength to hoist her dad onto the nearby sofa.

Waiting a while, she brought over a walker so her dad could use it to help stand. They were moving toward the bedroom when Paul arrived from church. He took my place beside Bill and they continued to lead him slowly to the bedroom, using a waist security belt to lift him onto the bed. This whole process took 20 minutes over a short distance. In bed, Bill argued and flailed his arms around. Becky assured me, "I can handle this. I'm okay." Bill was still wearing sweatpants and shirt he'd had on all day. Despite my desire to change his clothes, Becky insisted he could sleep in what he was wearing.

Bill slept all night, never getting out of bed. By 9:15 Monday morning, Bill remained in bed but not asleep. I was unsure how to get him into dry clean clothes. But I was able to help change his clothes with great effort and no complaint from Bill.

Monday afternoon Paul came from church with a borrowed wheelchair. Bill did not resist sitting in the wheelchair, and the first day went smoothly with Bill sitting at his computer and my pushing him to the table for meals. The second day proved difficult. Bill leaned over in the wheelchair all day, while we kept him strapped in. Glen M., associate pastor at church, visited in our living room, and while Glen talked, Bill did not respond. He stayed bent over. If I tried to straighten him, he returned to the same bent position. Pastor Glen told me later that he thought Bill might be tired and yet ready to meet Jesus.

That evening at supper, Bill's head stayed bent over near the table and he took little nourishment. He neither fed himself nor allowed me to feed him. Becky suggested we could use pureed foods if we were going to attempt to feed her dad. Later that evening with helpers, Paul exchanged our queen-sized bed for two twin-sized beds from the basement. We got Bill into bed, and we both slept well.

All the next two days, Bill stayed in bed, sleeping most of the time. I brought him meals and yet he ate little. Rob H., senior pastor from church, visited Bill in our bedroom, read Scripture, and prayed. Both in the afternoon and at bedtime, Becky helped with changing her dad's brief and clothes.

In-home Hospice Care

Becky phoned a friend who had experience with end-of-life care. When Becky described her dad's condition, the friend suggested calling hospice as our best choice. Becky relayed the conversation and we agreed. The next day Becky phoned a hospice agency nearby, recommended by Aleen. We set a time to have an admission nurse visit that same day. Our decision to contact hospice came after Bill's three falls (Friday, Saturday, and Sunday), followed by two days in a wheelchair and then two days in bed.

2-23-24—The admissions nurse arrived from Main Street Hospice to explain their services and our rights, getting my signature on legal papers. She also conducted an evaluation of Bill's condition. Two main issues qualified Bill for hospice care: poor mobility and lack of reasonable communication. He also was not eating well.

The nurse and Becky changed Bill's brief while he stayed in bed. He was not cooperative, flailing his arms and trying to hit the nurse. I was actually glad she was able to witness his anger. She took Bill's vital signs, even measuring his upper arm so the assigned hospice nurse could use that to document any loss of muscle mass. She left supplies: briefs, disposable bed pads, and sponges on a stick to use in giving Bill some water. Although long, the session was thorough and helpful. She scheduled Bill's hospice nurse, Steve, to visit twice a week. Confident, I knew in-home hospice care would be our best choice, and I expressed my gratitude.

The admissions nurse ordered a hospital bed, delivered and set up early the same evening. Thus Paul and Becky transported Bill from the twin bed he hadn't left for three days to the hospital bed. It was quite a feat but comical, as Bill snored through it all. I drove to the CVS 24-hour drugstore and picked up two new medications: one for anxiety and one for pain. All other medications were stopped. We gave Bill the anxiety medication 30 minutes before we changed his brief, and he was more cooperative. The first night in the hospital bed we both slept well, but I had to adjust to the squeaky noise of the air mattress as rotating cables filled with air, designed to prevent bed sores.

When reporting Bill's progress to family and friends, most were surprised at the rapid decline which led us to start in-home hospice care. All expressed concern and a promise to pray. Becky said her dad's progression through the advanced stage of Alzheimer's seemed like he had stepped off a cliff. His early stage had been fairly brief (a few years); the moderate over eight years, but the advanced stage would pass quickly.

Throughout this sudden change, Bill slept all night and most of the day. He rarely spoke. When awake, he allowed me to spoon-feed him either yogurt, applesauce, or pudding, mainly to hide his pills in soft food. He even drank water (definitely not his favorite beverage) with the use of the sponge on a paper stick. I often had to ask him to open his mouth and let go of the stick, because he bit down while sucking the water. Unique drinking method.

2-26-24—While Bill remained complacent during the first two times Becky and I changed his brief, he became agitated and combative from then on. He yelled, striking out with his arms, and wanted us to leave him alone. He tried to bite Becky and would twist and squeeze her fingers. Once when he gritted his teeth at Becky, she smiled, leaned over, and said to her dad, "You don't scare me one bit."

We tried various time frames with the distance between the anxiety medication and changing Bill's brief, but nothing helped. Thus, this twice-daily procedure became unpleasant, to say the least. After finishing one change of his brief, Bill lifted both arms in the air. Becky smiled as she said, "He's praising the Lord we are finally leaving him alone."

I marveled at how Becky moved from being a daughter to acting as her dad's nurse. Yes, her training kicked in, and I should not worry about Bill hurting her. She said, "I've been treated worse" (when a hospital nurse). She corrected me if I shouted "no" at him, and she protected me from his flailing arms. Advised by the nurse, Becky called her dad by name, Bill, in order to keep her care from being personal. At bedtime, Paul helped Becky pull Bill back up in bed onto his pillow. We were together, and we received Becky's and Paul's compassionate care.

2-27-24—Several phone calls helped arrange the visits from Main Street Hospice staff. Steve, Bill's hospice nurse, came in the mornings twice a week. The first day they also scheduled visits with a CNA, social worker, and chaplain, not at the same time. In one full day they introduced me to all the aspects of the hospice care team.

Mid-morning I fed Bill some yogurt (with two pills) and sponges of water. While he slept, I often sat at my desk to read and write. The hospice pharmacy service delivered medications, and Becky explained their purpose or function. Each day I waited until Becky came home from working in the church kitchen so she could help change Bill's brief.

2-28-24—The hospice nurse, Steve, and the aide (CNA) provided professional and gentle care with helpful exchange of information. Bill's vital signs remained in the normal range. When I asked the nurse about a time frame for Bill's end of life. Steve estimated "weeks, not months." My sister Martha defined "close" as "our being on this side of eternity, but an opening or beginning for Bill on the other side." Well-spoken from one who had experienced her husband's death.

The aide's duties included changing Bill's brief, bathing him, and giving oral care. She did all this with efficiency and compassion, but during her first visit she experienced Bill's combativeness. I provided soap, towel, and a clean T-shirt which we cut straight up the back to the neckband for easier handling.

3-1-24—During one of Steve's visits, Bill's BP was 160/110, a high diastolic, but all other vital signs were in normal range. Anna, our granddaughter in Tennessee, arrived that weekend. She not only expressed love for her grandpa, but gave helpful, experienced care as a psychiatric nurse. We sat on opposite sides of her grandpa's hospital bed and spent time rehearsing memories.

I contacted three pastors, friends in the Emmaus community, and requested their participation with Bill's memorial service when the time came. All agreed that World Gospel Church, Bill's last pastorate, would be the best location. I emailed the church and Callahan Funeral Home (both in Terre Haute, Indiana) about services we would need soon.

3-2-24—Local grandkids arrived for brief visits with their grandpa: Stephen and Emily; Chrissa, Léo, and their daughter Joana. Our granddaughter, Sarah, along with Anna's triplets made video Face Time calls. Bill's face showed little recognition, for he hadn't talked much in three days. Bill kept his eyes open most of the day. I sat on my twin bed and sent text messages to family and friends, receiving their confirmation of concern and prayer.

3-3-24—Sunday morning I fed Bill some yogurt with two pills, but he had difficulty swallowing. This proved to be his last day with food. Becky spoke to me about her dad's living will: no nourishment or extreme procedures to lengthen time before death. I phoned Main Street Hospice about this change, and they instructed me to crush the Ativan and Haldol, mix with water and give with a syringe in his mouth. Becky administered the medications since I wasn't comfortable with the syringe method. We added another medication before changing his brief. Due to his trouble with swallowing, we omitted his two medications prescribed as anti-depressants, but we crushed the tablet prescribed for anxiety to administer with water in a syringe.

3-4-24—I texted our longtime friend, a graduate from the high school in D'Iberville, Mississippi, where Bill taught English the first two years of our marriage. These graduates had continually been in touch with us over the 64 years since our time in Mississippi. Shirley R. has been my main contact person, and she responded with concern and a promise to alert the other former students.

Today I waited as our pastor arrived at our home. Later I waited on a visit from our oldest son Bill Jr., serving a Nazarene church in Ohio. Waiting became my theme; yet it was an actively prolonged process as Bill lingered on this side of eternity. This was not pleasant for any of us. During the day I continued to sit on my bed and read, pausing often to watch Bill and talk to him, even though he didn't respond much.

Contacts with Family

3-5-24—Bill Jr. arrived from Ohio and stayed three days. Each day we sat on either side of his dad's hospital bed, reminiscing and talking over future plans. I gleaned from his experience in speech pathology, working in a nursing home, and serving as a pastor. I took a photo of him with his dad, as I did with other visits from family.

3-6-24—Wednesday Bill's breathing became shallow. In the morning we could hear what's often referred to as the "death rattle" when he breathed. I phoned hospice and the nurse arrived for an extra visit. Steve hugged me, saying it would be soon and I should contact family members. He planned to come again the next day. Bill's heart was strong; blood pressure faint; breathing shallow and labored. Steve advised Becky to give oral Morphine with a syringe every two hours.

3-7-24—Bill Jr. returned home Thursday morning, and he later wrote, "After listening to Dad's lungs with a stethoscope, the rattles in his lungs suggested his death would be near. I didn't say anything about my assumption; I didn't want to create a sense of panic or dread. I drove home, glad to have had time with Mom and Dad in those concluding days of his life, knowing the best was yet to be. I focused on getting home in anticipation of turning around almost immediately to return with Rhonda. I found it easy to step away from the 'shadow' of Dad with little remorse. I knew him as a devoted Christian. My grief happened several years ago; but that day I felt relief."

That same day my friend Donna Dene E. visited briefly in the afternoon. She sat by the hospital bed and talked to us. Bill looked at her but didn't talk. She returned home, grateful for her time with us.

Our son John arrived from Kentucky, and his son Wes also came from north of Indianapolis. I phoned our grandson Eric, John's son in Tennessee, and we had a Face Time video call with the family: his wife, Carrianna, and their four children. Later I received word the kids prayed for their great-grandpa at bedtime.

That evening our family—Becky, Paul, John, Wes, and I—visited in the bedroom. Then we all sat around the dining room table to talk. I kept a baby monitor handy when not in the bedroom. I viewed Bill as he occasionally kicked his legs under the blanket, and I'd see his chest move as he breathed.

Around 9:30, Wes got up from the table, because he needed to go home. He walked to the bedroom to tell his grandpa goodbye, but quickly returned to say, "I don't think he's breathing." We all went to the bedroom where Becky listened to her dad's heart with her stethoscope, put her cheek up to his mouth, and held his wrist to get a pulse. Nothing. She said, "He's gone."

Several times earlier I would be on one side of Bill's bed, kiss his cheek, and say, "I love you." While breathing was shallow with the "death rattle," his mouth stayed wide open and I could not close it. Earlier that evening my last words to Bill were, "You are working too hard; you are laboring. Just let go. Just go." He did, but not while I was in the room. Surprisingly, this didn't upset me, even though I had imagined being by his side when he took his last breath.

I moved to the side of Bill's hospital bed and touched his cheek, both cold and stiff. He no longer resided in the shell of his body. His soul, his true self, had quickly entered the presence of his Savior. Heaven bound most of his life, now he arrived there. I recalled something Mary DeMuth said on her podcast: "What's broken is made whole in heaven." Bill was not only Home, but his broken brain and body were now whole, new, perfect.

Our family stood around the bed a short while, and then I phoned Main Street Hospice to report Bill had stopped breathing. Their 24-7 operator called a staff nurse, and she phoned back soon, saying she would be here as soon as possible.

During his years of dementia I had found the reality of the term ambiguous loss. He was present but away. It's a term used with "both . . . and." My husband had been both here and gone. Now with his death, the loss was final. Memories and influence are all that's left from his life of 88 plus years. I took comfort in the assurance that "Precious in the sight of the LORD is the death of his faithful servants" (Psalm 116:15).

The hospice nurse arrived and confirmed the time of death as 10:30 PM, Thursday, March 7, 2024, to be recorded on his death certificate.

The nurse bathed Bill and put him in a clean brief and T-shirt. I phoned Callahan Funeral Home in Terre Haute, and David C., the director, spoke with both the hospice nurse and me. He informed me someone would arrive within two hours to transport Bill's body.

Since Becky and Paul had to work the next day, they went to bed. Wes returned home, and John stayed with me. While waiting, I busied myself by tidying up the room and packing items we no longer needed. When our son Bill Jr. was here, he had helped me gather the clothes his dad would wear after the embalming and before being placed in the casket. I had chosen a suit, white dress shirt, my favorite of his many ties, and dress shoes—items Bill often wore when he preached. I had these items ready for the funeral home staff when they arrived.

Two middle-aged men, dressed in suits and ties, arrived around midnight and gently moved Bill's body from the hospital bed to a gurney and then to their van. Respectful and efficient, they even asked if I preferred to leave the room. I stayed and soon handed them the bag I had set aside with Bill's clothes. John helped, then headed to a guest room in the basement. After everyone left, I showered and got in bed, alone in the room with an empty hospital bed. Without any tension, sleep came peacefully.

Making Arrangements

3-8-24—The day after. Multiple phone calls became necessary—funeral home, hospice, pastors, family, and friends. The same young man who delivered the hospital bed came to retrieve it, and John assisted him. Using Bill's resume, I wrote the obituary to submit to the funeral home, newspapers, and schools. The funeral director and I agreed to make arrangements using phone calls and emails, so it wasn't necessary to travel to Terre Haute. I answered his questions about embalming, a floral spray on the casket, and scheduled times for family viewing, visitation, and memorial service. While still in bed one morning, I rehearsed terminology such as visitation and viewing, related to the funeral. Were there better substitutes? Probably not, so we dealt with these awkward terms.

Our son Tom arrived, and he and John stayed the week between their dad's death and his memorial service. This gave us time to attend to items needing to be settled, write a list of contacts, and when solutions resolved questions. Tom had helped his mother-in-law with such issues after her husband died, so he knew the term "durable" in front of Power of Attorney meant I continued to be POA after Bill's death.

John offered help with my finances, knowing income would decrease from Social Security. And the question arose whether I'd receive a survivor benefit with Bill's pension from the United Methodist Church. Finding contact information, I began to phone and write agencies who could supply answers. Some would need Bill's death certificate. The car was in my name only, so that was easily settled. The banks would need to adjust joint accounts to single and Bill's IRA accounts transferred to me. Even voter registration needed to be notified. Our attorney confirmed that a probate would not be necessary. After a call to one doctor, I found I didn't need to phone them all. The system in place alerted them of Bill's death.

I phoned World Gospel Church, along with Paul Z., Gary S., and Dan W., the three pastor friends who would conduct the memorial service. Prior to our move to Indianapolis, we had filed decisions with the funeral home. This made final arrangements easier. We decided on asking our grandsons to be pallbearers, and with five in attendance and agreeable; Bill Jr. would be the needed sixth pallbearer.

3-15-24—I decided to hold Bill's memorial service on Friday 15th of March at World Gospel Church (WGC). Grandkids I had not seen in quite a long time arrived at our home, and I noticed how much they had grown. One grandson took time off from work and rented a car. Another grandson brought his dog, a former police K-9. Young cousins especially enjoyed being together.

At my request, the funeral home placed the open casket at the front in the church sanctuary. Family members had opportunity to view the body before friends arrived. The family appreciated the light lunch prepared by church members. When it became time, our four children and I formed a receiving line to the left of the casket. Other family members sat in several front row pews and milled around. This time presented an extra special family gathering.

Friends from the community soon arrived, signed the guest register in back, and moved up front toward the casket and our family. Persons who came to pay their respects were those who had attended WGC when Bill was their pastor. In addition, members of FLCC, along with friends from the local Emmaus community, and friends from Indianapolis, attended, including the two pastors from Southport Presbyterian Church. Some folks arrived from a distance, such as Bonnie B., a long-time friend from Asbury College in Wilmore, Kentucky. Hugs and greetings from these friends brought joy and satisfaction, as I recognized Bill's influence on their lives. I observed how our Asian friends spent more time at the casket, visibly appreciative of Bill's ministries in the church and community.

Sitting on the front pew, my family surrounding me, I listened to the memorial service, the structure and Scriptures which Bill and I had planned while still living in Terre Haute. We had chosen our three pastor friends to officiate, and I included Ben B., the new pastor at WGC. Musicians we knew when Bill pastored there also participated, playing instruments (Mallory N. and Mimi M.) and leading hymns (Andy M.) for those in attendance. The singing sounded robust.

The service opened with a surprise: a video of our German friend, Stefanie, playing "The Steadfast Love of the Lord" on her recorder, in tribute to her former pastor while attending graduate studies at Rose Hulman in Terre Haute. Unknown to me, Bill years ago had requested Andy, song leader and friend, to sing a special solo at his funeral, "The Lord Is My Light." Later I found out the sound engineer, David P., recorded the whole service, making it available on WGC's website. It became a way to share the service with people who could not attend. When the service ended, people filed out past the casket and I received more greetings.

An earlier forecast predicted rain, but when we arrived at the cemetery the weather cooperated. They erected a tent and I sat near the casket among a few family members and friends. Pastor Dan closed in prayer and committed Bill's body to the ground. Of course, his real self already donned a new body once he left his earthly tent. Some of the family climbed up the hill to see the gravestone, not yet engraved with the date of death. The funeral director contacted me later when the date had been added. A friend, Kathy D., volunteered to come occasionally to make sure the gravestone and grass around it were kept neat.

The funeral home attendants loaded flowers and plants into cars heading to Indianapolis. Back home with family, we were greeted by friends from Southport Presbyterian Church who had assembled food for our family's evening meal. Our friend, Bonnie B., from Asbury College joined us. We talked over memories, and I answered questions about Bill's last days and his hospice care. Some of the family stayed overnight and left to return home in the wee hours of the next morning. Their visits ended too soon, but it was part of our closure.

Questions for Reflection:

1. What difficult decisions did you have to make for the closing of life?

2. Have you prepared ahead of time a memorial service and made funeral arrangements?
3. How are the family getting involved? Do you feel in-control or not?

PART IV

Focus on Forever—
A New Chapter

During my grief journey, I've thought deeply about the word "loss." It's what people say when expressing sympathy, "I'm sorry for your loss." Admittedly, there is loss on my part. Bill is no longer beside me in our queen-sized bed or sitting in the passenger seat of the car as I drive to church and errands. No longer is he pointing to our clock on the wall to alert me when it's mealtime. In church I now sit in the third seat from the aisle where Bill sat, leaving two seats for Becky and Paul.

Bill, however, is not lost. I know where he is. I do not need to find him and reclaim a "lost object." He is with his Savior and Lord, rejoicing in heaven. One day I will join him.

In his 2002 journal, Bill wrote about loss and it fits aptly here with my grief journey. "We so often take relationships casually, until we face their loss. The loss always leaves a hole, which may be partially filled with new relationships. But the deeper the relationship, the more remaining emptiness. I understand why, as we grow older, the holes increase and the empty places leave a longing for a day of restoration."

The biblical truth of bodily resurrection is more real and palatable now that Bill has made the transfer. The third stanza of *Jesus Loves Me* sums up what's ahead: "Jesus loves me! He will stay close beside me on my way. He's prepared a home for me, and someday His face I'll see. Yes, Jesus loves me!" (Anna B. Warner).

Ambiguous loss impacted our lives during those many years of dementia—Bill being present but away. No longer present, he is now away and forever. My grief began not with his death but grew as dementia increased slowly and then dramatically. I have moments when I find myself looking for him and even wishing he were here. Those moments surprise me, such as when in bed I cough and look over to see if I've disturbed Bill. When shopping at Walmart, I wish he were along pushing the cart; and during laundry day his help folding clothes would be appreciated. Simple remembrances.

I look to Bill's chair at the dinner table, and perhaps surprisingly I do not wish to have back the man who sat there. I do miss my husband who sat at our breakfast room table in Terre Haute—before dementia stole his brain and personality. At first I occupied his seat at our dining room table, but it didn't feel natural, so I moved to my usual chair. It's all a matter of well-thought-through perspective.

For the most part I'm relieved Bill is no longer suffering in this earthly life. And I'm no longer weighed down with the personal difficulties of his condition. Our arguments and my frustration with caregiving have passed. I'm grateful how God guided me through it, but I'm actually glad the caregiving chores are over.

Doing the Usual

3-17-24—Two days after Bill's funeral, it was Sunday morning and I did the usual. I attended Sunday school and worship service at church. As I looked at my calendar, that's all I'd written to do. During Sunday school I answered a question that seemed to relate to how Bill's body was cold and stiff.

On Monday I also did the usual. I attended a scheduled Zoom meeting of writers in BookCamp. I took care of some laundry which I'd put off from the previous week. I noticed my wash loads were reduced by more than half. I opened the linen closet and looked at the towels. I can use a blue towel now. Those had hung on the towel rack for Bill's use, but no longer a needed consideration. With Bill's death, changes have come in small increments and often subtle and insignificant within the larger picture.

Tuesday we held our monthly Zoom siblings meeting. Because my two sisters and my brother could not attend Bill's funeral, I provided a summary and promised to send them the link to the memorial service online. Already God's peace ruled my heart and mind.

Wednesday morning I met a writer friend, Beth S., for breakfast at Cracker Barrel. I had forgotten to contact her about Bill's death, and she heard only recently. Again I shared Bill's last days, and again God's peace enveloped me closely. It is impossible to express adequately the understanding of peace that comes only from God. Beth and I also enjoyed our time to catch up on other family events.

3-21-24—Thursday I was not out of bed until 10 o'clock, and ate breakfast at 11:00. I spent the early part of the afternoon working without a break at the computer. At 4:30 I found myself face down on my desk. Did I fall asleep or faint? I decided to eat some protein-rich food. When I told Becky, she suggested I call my doctor due to my concern.

During a visit with the nurse practitioner (NP), she requested I check my blood pressure and pulse every day. After I reported a low pulse rate, she scheduled an Echocardiogram and to wear a heart monitor for seven days. Results were normal, but as advised I made an appointment with a cardiologist who scheduled a chemical stress test and a MRI. When he went over test results, he found no heart problems. I settled on *my* twofold diagnosis: I needed to eat the day I passed out, and it could also be related to weariness and grief. The cardiologist prescribed new medications to regulate my blood pressure.

3-22-24—I began the task of contacting two banks about switching *our* joint accounts to *my* single account. With the local bank it could not be changed until 45 days after Bill's death. I phoned Social Security to determine the amount I'd now receive. A problem arose: the package from the funeral home, including Bill's death certificates, got lost in the mail and didn't arrive for two weeks after the mailing date. I needed those official documents in making various contacts to certify Bill's death. Finding out my adjusted Social Security income and that I qualified for survivor benefits through Bill's United Methodist Church pension took time, but the knowledge brought relief.

3-27-24—Becky informed me about small group opportunities at church, something I'd not done while Bill was alive. I chose to join GriefShare, meeting on Wednesdays for thirteen weeks. The leader, Aleen, approved my joining the third session. During those sessions I soon learned how each person's grief journey varies. Some of the topics (anger and resentment) didn't seem applicable with my present-day trouble (although I'd dealt with these during Bill's years of dementia). Attending the group sessions and personally going through the workbook aided my healing journey. Interaction among members also gave avenues for increased empathy toward others.

3-31-24—Easter Sunday. Resurrection life I now viewed with fresh meaning. I say that with a lump in my throat and a few tears. One surprise during my current grief journey has been the absence of crying. Most moist eyes come when people related how Bill greatly influenced their lives. They gave oral expressions or wrote notes in the vast number of sympathy cards I received.

At first I focused more on what was no longer necessary, such as the duties of caregiving, a relief. I no longer dread Saturdays with the frustrations involved in attempting to persuade Bill to shower. Reading a report on caregiving, I recognized my method did not help reduce Bill's resistance to bathing. The Harvard Medical School's instruction sheet starts with "avoid discussing whether a bath is needed." It closes with: "If a person refuses to get into the tub or shower, be flexible and suggest an alternative. If all else fails, try again later." I regret that had not been my approach.

Absent are our times of angry interchange and Bill's confusion with Sundowner's Syndrome. Most of my tears were shed *during* caregiving—when upset with myself and how I reacted unkindly to Bill's words and actions. All of those challenges and regrets are now in the past and I choose not to linger there. I'm determined not to dwell on regrets or shame. A friend assured me I took care of regrets through confession to God on a daily basis. God forgave me of those inappropriate reactions and ill feelings, moments of anger or neglect of good care.

Knowing the negatives have been present in my mind, I now aim to focus on the positives, the good memories. I'm remembering how Bill liked to tease me, do a jig in the doorway, and enter a room with a smile saying, "I love you," while throwing kisses my way. I recall those times Bill listened to music on a CD, not singing, but clucking his tongue to the melody, anticipating the notes to follow. He enjoyed meals, often helping his plate before we said grace. He was happy living in our home with family and visits from friends.

Wednesdays I continue to listen to his podcast, and I'm reminded of the years he had the ability to study God's Word and the privilege to preach the gospel message. The tech team agreed to continue downloading his sermons. Erik T. and Michael G. recorded a brief announcement about Bill's death and our intention to proceed with the weekly podcast. Listening to podcast episodes, I see Bill's photo on my phone, and I'm not sad. I enjoy his past messages and praise God that I had the joy of being my pastor's wife. I sometimes picture myself sitting in a pew at World Gospel Church, hearing Bill preach, learning more about God and His Word.

I agree with a message sent to Bill years ago by a young friend, Kristin S.:

"For all the sermons you have written and preached,

For the many people you so vigilantly teach,

For all the broken hearts you so carefully mend,

For all the small seedlings you so gently tend,

For all the lost souls you so willingly lead home,

Thank you, Pastor."

The Real Angst

4-2-24—Hearing Ephesians 6:12 brought me back to those times when my anger surfaced due to Bill's confused mental state and my reaction to his loss. "Our struggle is not against flesh and blood, but against...the powers of this dark world."

Bill was not the enemy, but his disease represented a force of darkness, the true cause of my angst. During those times, reality brought me anguish, resulting in guilt and crying episodes. Now I gradually allow those troubling times to rest in the past, having accepted God's mercy and forgiveness.

I busied myself going through Bill's belongings, distributing some items to family and placing in bags items to donate. Bill's personal belongings and tools of his trade (preaching) have not been distributed as quickly as I'd expected. Family members didn't take many items after the funeral. Some items they did want, but more was left behind. Since our first son has the same name as his dad and same initials, his choices were appropriate, such as a briefcase with the initials WBC. One grandson, Tommy C., wanted his grandpa's plastic stays for dress shirts. Unusual request, but I liked that. Two grandsons-in-law, Ted V., and Michael R., chose several ties, but plenty were left. I recall when my father died, each sibling wanted one of his handkerchiefs as a memento.

Becky has been helpful with this task, as she asked friends and posted items online. A sack of blue jeans went to her friend who is Bill's size. Paul brought a box of dress clothes to an organization supplying pastors' needs in another country. Some clothes and shoes we boxed for a local mission. Someone online requested Bill's computer and picked it up. His desk also went to a man in the community. A slow process, but eventually most items have found a good home. I returned unused packaged items for incontinence and received a refund.

4-6-24—Considering the word *caregiving*, I believe it has two aspects: the caring for another and the giving of care. While I did care for Bill as my husband who dealt with dementia, and I did my best (somewhat) to meet his needs, I am grateful we had time together. Some caregiving required hard work and others met with opposition on my part as well as from Bill.

I recall what Bill said about his episode with depression during the end of his time at Asbury College. He would not wish it on others, but he wouldn't trade what he learned from his experience. It allowed him to relate better with others during counseling sessions. That is how I evaluate my years of caregiving. I don't wish it on anyone, but I highly value the experience and can now relate better with others during their similar journeys.

I've asked myself, "What do I miss now Bill is no longer alive?" My immediate answer is one word: presence. I miss Bill being near as well as dear to me for over 66 years. Most of my life, Bill was my husband, father to our four children, grandpa to our ten grandkids and thirteen great-grandkids, *and* he was my pastor who taught me about God and His will.

As I wrote in a card to Bill many years ago, I can also adopt it now with sincerity: "You've stuck with me, held onto me, stayed true, protected, provided, and kept your promise, loved and nurtured me and our children. I've been included in your life and I look forward to the future with you. I love you dearly."

Bill's presence in my life I compare to my relationship with Jesus. I would not want to exist one day, one moment, without the presence of the Lord in my life. He is my Savior and Friend. My relationship with Jesus sustains me daily in every way possible. Not having the presence of my husband is difficult, but not having God's presence would be far worse. Life will be good whatever the future holds. My testimony is found in the hymn *A Wonderful Savior* by Fanny Crosby: "He hideth my life in the depths of His love and covers me there with His hand."

I rest my future in God's hands, because there I am safe and secure.

Questions for Reflection:

1. My grief journey began when dementia started, not when my husband died. Can you

relate? Isn't your grief journey different? And different is alright.

2. How did life change for you? Are you seeking good help? Perhaps you could join GriefShare or another support group.

Quotes and References

Unless otherwise indicated, all Scripture quotations are taken from THE HOLY BIBLE, NEW INTERNATIONAL VERSION ® Copyright © 1973, 1978, 1984, 2011 by Biblica, Inc.™ Used by permission. All rights reserved worldwide.

pp. 2-3—*Blank Stares* by musician Jay Allen, used by permission

p. 38—Quote attributed to Robert Louis Stevenson

p. 50—*New Every Day* © 2018 by Dave Meurer, Revell, division of Baker Publishing Group

p. 51—*Second Forgetting* © 2014 by Dr. Benjamin T. Mast, Zondervan

p. 51 & 151—*Loving Someone Who Has Dementia,* Pauline Boss, PhD, © 2011, Jossey-Bass Publisher

p. 51—Quote attributed to Charles R. Swindoll

p. 78—*The Bard and the Bible,* March 10, © 2016 by Bob Hostetler, Worthy Inspired

p. 90—*We Have Seen God's Glory*—Steve Green

p. 99—A. W. Tozer, quote from *Worship, the Missing Jewel* in *The Pursuit of God Bible,* NIV, © 2011 by Biblica, Inc., Hendrickson Marketing LLC, p. 1366

p. 99—A. W. Tozer, quote from *The Counselor* in *The Pursuit of God Bible,* NIV, © 2011 by Biblica, Inc., Hendrickson Marketing LLC, p. 920

pp. 102–103—Introduction to a Bible study, led by Beth Summitt, Indianapolis, IN

p. 125—Source of quote from Marcus Aurelius: AARP Magazine, Dec. 2024/Jan. 2025

p. 128—Allie Sgro, "Where I Need To Be," Guideposts, Aug/Sept 2022, p. 43. Reprinted with permission from *Guideposts.*

p. 147–148—Rebecca Anne Coker Gearhart, post from her Facebook page

p. 148—Alzheimer's Disease Research, BrightFocus Foundation Program, Clarksburg, MD—brightfocus.org/stopAD

pp. 149-150—Anna Coker Rhodes, letter she wrote about her grandpa

p. 151—*The Pilgrim's Progress* by John Bunyan

p. 151—*Journey with Bunyan's Pilgrim* by Ann L. Coker

p. 165—*Jesus Loves Me* by Anna B. Warner (public domain)

p. 167—*The Gift of Empathy* by Joel P. Bretscher and Kenneth C. Haugk, © 2023 by Stephen Ministries, St. Louis, MO

p. 169—*Daily Creative* © by Todd Henry, Oct. 4, p. 288, Sourcebooks, Simple Truths

pp. 175—"Living with Dementia" CereScan.com, later changed to HealthScan.com—https://www.alztennessee.org/uploads/Brochure%20PDFs/Ten%20Absolutes%20August%202017.pdf

p. 176—Quote by Cooper Esley at Southport Presbyterian Church, Indianapolis, IN

p. 180—Quote attributed to Ruth Graham about Billy Graham—https://time.com/archive/6922265/ruth-graham-soulmate-to-billy-dies/

pp. 184—*Daily Creative* © by Todd Henry, Nov 11, p. 327, Sourcebooks, Simple Truths

p. 186—*Tar-Baby and Other Rhymes of Uncle Remus* (1904) by Joel Chandler Harris

p. 236—Excerpt from Mary DeMuth's podcast Pray Every Day (5/1/24)

p. 246—*Jesus Loves Me*—3rd stanza—Anna B. Warner (public domain) pp. 250–251—"How to take care of a person with dementia," by Beverly Merz, Harvard Medical School, Harvard Health Publishing, July 20, 2017

p. 255—*A Wonderful Savior*—Fanny Crosby (public domain)

Insights for Caregivers

Caregiving for someone with dementia can push your limits. It's demanding. It means you put someone else's needs above your own. You have no room for selfishness, yet you need self-care and self-control. Caregiving refines your character. You have the privilege of caring for someone who needs you. This high calling proves your love while giving opportunities to practice the fruit of the Spirit.

Following are my 12 helpful tips for caregivers.

1. Expect your need for change. It's up to the caregiver to make the adjustments. Your loved one is not able. Their logic and understanding continue to decrease.

2. Find jobs and activities for your loved one. When they are not suited at one task, look for another. Most dementia patients like tactile tasks such as folding laundry, helping to make up the bed, or setting the table for dinner. Most dementia patients sincerely want to be useful.

3. Know that your loved one will decrease in functions during each stage of dementia. With loss of identity, changes in personality are observed. Your loved one may act more like a toddler than an adult, so accept those changes graciously. The difference: toddlers are learning skills while dementia patients are losing what has been learned.

4. Accept the fact that your loved one will not get better. No one has been "healed" of dementia. Facing reality is difficult, but the process can be rewarding for you and your loved one.

5. Take care of yourself. That involves physical, mental, and relational care. Eat well, get adequate sleep, keep your mind sharp, and relate regularly with family and friends.

6. Admit you need help in various ways. The type varies with each person and situation. In-home care is good, but not always the best for everyone. Keep your family members informed and involved. They could be your best supporters.

7. Identify the core of your loved one. Was he or she a good provider or a person who have been in authority? That may explain some of their behavior. Concentrate on the truth. Not everything you want is necessary.

8. Rediscover what your loved one likes to do. If that's talking, listen with interaction. If it's games on the computer or being read to, take time to include those activities. Invite family and friends to visit, and try to get your loved one's attention onto others.

9. Embrace flexibility. Certain words, especially negative ones, will likely cause an unworthy reaction from your loved one. One difficult task is requesting their attention to matters of personal hygiene care. Asking is often heard as a command and not supportive. If your loved one refuses a request, don't insist. Try again later.

10. Choose what's recognized as loving. Relate with empathy, trying to imagine how you would respond in their situation. Reflect on what's good, what you appreciate about their new condition, such as a change in showing affection.

11. Look for the humor in many situations. A silly act or even words lost in meaning can have a good effect on both you and your loved one. Enjoy those moments.

12. Find the benefits you can glean from hardships. Difficult situations can often result in good happening unexpectedly. Also, prayer helps in every situation.

Questions for Reflection:

1. Were any of these insights helpful? Did any specifics relate well to your situation? If so, what helped you the most? If not, what would you have changed?
2. What insights would you add? What have you found out through your own experiences?
3. How would you share these with others going through the journey of caregiving?

Recommended Reading for Caregivers

New Every Day by Dave Meurer, Revell, division of Baker Publishing Group, 2018. The author was caregiver with his wife for her mother. His words "new every day" became mine.

The Second Forgetting by Dr. Benjamin Mast, author and physician, Zondervan Publisher, 2014. "Caregiving provides us with an opportunity to grow in grace."

Loving Someone Who Has Dementia: How to Find Hope While Coping with Stress and Grief by Pauline Boss, PhD, Jossey-Bass Publishers, 2011. She introduces the term "ambiguous loss" and how to live with it.

In Lieu of Flowers: A Conversation for the Living by Nancy Cobb, Pantheon Books, 2001. "Grief is an integral part of life. We have lived and loved, surely we will grieve."

Where the Light Gets In: Losing My Mother Only to Find Her Again by Kimberly Williams-Paisley, Three Rivers Press, 2017. A heartfelt memoir of a daughter relating her mother's crippling process from a rare form of dementia.

The Long Run by Richard Sherry © 2020. A personal story as caregiver for his wife with physical and mental issues.

Grace for Expected Journey by Deborah Barr, Moody Publishers, 2018. A 60-day devotional for Alzheimer's disease and other dementia caregivers.

Confronting Dementia: A Husband's Journey as an Alzheimer's Caregiver by Stu Ervay, EABooks Publishing, 2021—This memoir includes the author's experience along with several imaginative stories he creates of couples, adding his comments.

A Journey of Faith by Edward Grinnan, Guideposts Books, 2023. A son's story of his mother's

Alzheimer's disease and his search for answers, which includes his own love story.

Grieving God's Way: The Path to Lasting Hope and Healing by Margaret Brownley, Thomas Nelson Publisher, 2012. A 90-day devotional that includes Scripture and quotes from resources.

Acknowledgements

My first thanks must go to my Savior and constant Friend, Jesus Christ. He has been the best caregiver through my whole life. I would not have survived the caregiving journey without Him. Jesus was my constant help, especially when I had to learn lessons repeatedly. Whenever I faced the real angst against my role, I came to God needing His forgiveness and direction to confront the next challenge. Through all the ups and downs, the in and out of obedience, Jesus was there for me, and I'm grateful for His guidance and stability to press on.

To my children I extend love and thanks for all their support. Becky especially provided what I needed to hear, even when I resisted her advice. She and her husband, Paul, extended gracious and compassionate care throughout the years of indecision about our move and then while we lived together in Indianapolis. While I acted as Bill's main caregiver, Becky, RN, gave of her time, energy, and skills to make our journey one that resounded with joy when we faced head-on decisions. She had the courage to tell me what I needed to do and stood with me through it all. Becky also contributed to editing this memoir, adding her medical knowledge and helping me choose the best words. Our sons, Bill Jr., John, and Tom, came when needed and kept in touch throughout the whole journey. Their attention to our needs proved valuable.

I'm also thankful for the editorial assistance from Rachel Hills and Arlean Selvy, and for all who read rough drafts, giving comments about needed changes, as well as encouragement. A special thanks goes to Robin Black who worked on the format and submission. The finished product is because of the many who took time to assist me, and that includes those in BookCamp who took my writing seriously. Thanks.

About the Author

Ann L. Coker graduated from Asbury College, Wilmore, Kentucky, 20 years after completing high school in her hometown of Mobile, Alabama. Ann is an author and editor whose journalistic training started as managing editor (1981-84) of *Good News* magazine, founded by Charles Keysor, her journalism professor at Asbury College. Ann contributed annotations and topical notes for *The Woman's Study Bible*, NKJV, Thomas Nelson Publishers. She has written devotions for *Pathways*, *Opening the Word*, and *A Cup of Comfort*, along with articles for other periodicals. In 2023 Ann published her first book: *Journey with Bunyan's Pilgrim*.

When her husband, Bill Coker, developed Alzheimer's disease, Ann compiled and edited his pastoral sermons and prayers into books. As of 2025 she has overseen the publication of four books: *Words of Endearment; Prayers for the People; The Scandal of Christmas;* and *Let the Church Be the Church.* With a tech team who oversees Bill's podcast, Ann writes scripts for Words of Endearment with Bill Coker. Ann attends to a growing following of friends, connecting with emails and Facebook, and she regularly posts on her blog (www.abcoker. blog). In 2016 Ann completed assignments in Jerry Jenkins Writers Guild. Since 2019 she has maintained membership in BookCamp (Chad R. Allen, CEO). Ann is also a member of Heartland Writers Group in Indianapolis. She attends Southport Presbyterian Church in Indianapolis.

Ann and Bill have four adult children, ten grandchildren, and fifteen great-grandchildren. They both grew up along the Gulf Coast, later living in Mississippi, Kentucky, and Indiana for schooling and ministry positions. Bill died on March 7th of 2024 after 66 years of marriage, and Ann continues to live in Indianapolis with her married daughter and her husband. Ann's pastimes include journaling, reading, coloring, and creating greeting cards.